25th Edition
50 Years
of Publication

Ohio School Finance Blue Book

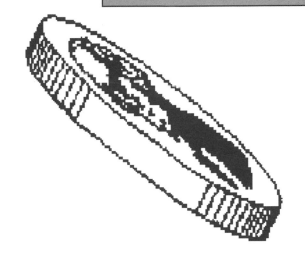

2022-2023 Edition
By Robert G. Stabile, Ph.D.
with Michael A. Rock, CPA, Ed.D.

About the Authors:

Robert G. Stabile has served Ohio education as a teacher and coach at Bedford High School, superintendent of schools at Manchester Local, Mayfield City and Berea City and as a Professor of Education at Franciscan University. He graduated from Miami University and earned M.A. and Ph.D. degrees from Kent State.

Dr. Stabile is the first recipient of the Dick Maxwell Ohio School Finance award, presented by the Buckeye Association of School Administrators in 2014.

Michael A. Rock received his Ed.D. from North Central University. He entered public service in 2005 as treasurer of Buckeye Local Schools after a career in public accounting. He is the current CFO Treasurer of Warrensville Heights City Schools and a leader in Ohio school finance activities.

Acknowledgments:

This is the 25th edition of the Ohio School Finance Blue Book. The book has been revised and updated every two years, following the adoption of a new **State** budget and changes to the school finance system made by the Legislature of the State of Ohio.

Appreciation is extended to the following individuals and organizations for their assistance in reviewing or providing information included in this edition:

Tom Ash, Director of Governmental Development,
    Buckeye Association of School Administrators.
Howard Fleeter, Education Tax Policy Institute
Richard Maxwell
Will Schwartz, Ohio School Boards Association
Scott Snyder, Treasurer, Mayfield City Schools
Office of Budget and Management
Legislative Service Commission
Ohio Department of Education
Ohio Department of Taxation
Cleveland Plain Dealer
Columbus Dispatch
Various Internet Sources

The 2022-2023 update to this book was provided by Mike Rock.

Table of contents

Introduction 1

Important concepts of local school finance 6

Raising funds for schools at the local level 23

Financing school construction 33

State support of education 40

Federal aid to education 53

School budget 59

Why do schools keep asking for more money? 71

Local voting decisions 82

The courts and school finance 84

Related school financial factors 94

Conclusion - Get involved 111

Glossary of Terms 113

Complexity Obscures Understanding

The Ohio school finance system has been described as the most complex in the nation. It is the aim of this book to help make that system understandable to the average citizen.

This handbook was written to provide basic information on Ohio school finance to all Ohio citizens; from students in colleges to school staff members, boards of education, parents, members of interested organizations, or just plain voting citizens who wish to acquire an understanding of the topic before casting their next ballot or forming an opinion on a local school issue.

The material is presented in a readable fashion, providing the basic concepts for the reader who wishes to understand the field, or a specific aspect, of Ohio school finance. In addition, it includes sufficient detail to make it a handy general reference source for school people, or for professors who are seeking a reasonably priced and easy to understand text for courses in school finance.

Introduction

Education in context

Education is the engine which has powered our nation to unprecedented levels of wealth and freedom. In our political system of representative democracy, which assures our freedoms, the most important office is that of "citizen," the voters with the ultimate power. Our sophisticated capitalistic economic system has created national wealth which is the envy of the world. Neither could function without a highly educated populace. Education is, and has been, the foundation upon which the greatness and well-being of America depends.

We are fortunate indeed that our founding fathers, led by Thomas Jefferson, saw the value of educating all the people. They believed that the ultimate power of society should reside with the people and that society must, as Jefferson felt, "inform their discretion by education." Jefferson also wrote, "The nation that wishes to be both ignorant and free, in a state of civilization, wants what never was and never will be."

Jefferson set the initial tone, which was carried on by following generations of educational, civic and political leaders. Over time a national consensus developed around three legal movements regarding treatment of our young people, which allowed us to develop the outstanding school system we have in America today:

- Child labor laws, which got children out of the workplace.
- Compulsory school attendance laws, which required our children to attend school, and
- Universal taxation for education, which pays to educate the children who are required to attend school.

Though we take all three for granted today, the issue of universal taxation for education remains very much alive, especially in the Ohio school finance system, where such a large percentage of the funding must be provided through the vote of the local citizens.

Free public education is far from free. Because education deals with two things people care deeply about - their children and their money - issues relating to school funding are hotly debated. Follow the General Assembly deliberations, or a school finance campaign in your local district, and you will likely see the following issues:

- How much free public education should the taxpayers provide?
- Are our schools using tax dollars to teach our children the right things?
- How much should free public education cost?
- How will the money available for education be divided?
- What form of taxation should be used to raise funds for education?
- Who will pay what part of the cost of free public education?
- Is the money available being used efficiently?

Why study Ohio school finance?

The financial commitment which taxpayers of Ohio make to educate our young people from kindergarten to grade 12 is enormous. There are about 1.7 million students in our 610 school districts; the education of each student is important. 139,000 active teachers have made the education of our young people their life's work. We now spend almost $20,000,000,000 (20 billion dollars) a year in tax money on public elementary and secondary school operations. The average cost per pupil in our public schools was $12,472 in FY2019. The cost of public education in Ohio continues to be the third largest State expenditure after Medicaid and General Government expenditures.

The economic impact of the public school district on the communities in which they are located is highly significant. It would not be uncommon for the local school district to employ the largest number of highly skilled and educated workers in the community. The school cafeterias may serve more meals than local restaurants. The district may operate the largest transportation system in the area. The district may be the largest owner of land and building used for education and related services.

Schools and the people employed by the schools are significant consumers of local goods and services, contributing to the local economy. In addition, local educators are woven into the fabric of the community, holding civic office, serving in volunteer organizations and supporting the community in many ways

School Finance is Part of a Bigger Budget Picture

The State general operating fund (GRF General Revenue Fund) is divided into six areas of expenditure (graph and table). The biggest State expenditure is now Medicaid (47% of the total GRF Fund), while Primary and Secondary Education is the second largest at 28%. In State, as in local budgeting, there is always external pressure to determine priorities as each recipient of funds works to convince decision makers of the importance of their function. Legislators have their own priorities and constituents to satisfy. The process is a result of an initial proposal by the Governor, amendments by the House of Representatives, amendments by the Senate, and then final approval by the Governor. The Governor has final veto powers on the budget. In addition, income factors, such as changes in tax law or the growth or reduction in certain tax bases have to be considered. Budgeting is complex. The latest biennial budget, HB110 is over 2,400 pages long.

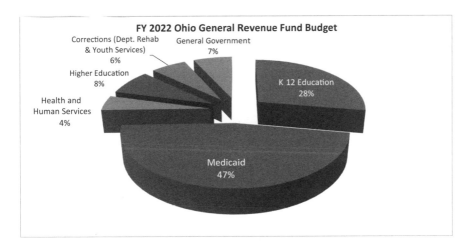

MainOperatingBudget
HouseBill110Budget(dollarsinmillions)

ProgramCategory	FY2021	FY2022	%change	FY2023	%change
K-12Education	$9,437.0	$9,803.9	3.7%	$9,749.0	-0.6%
Medicaid	$16,518.0	$16,441.3	-0.5%	$20,340.8	19.2%
Health	$1,367.0	$1,629.3	16.1%	$1,610.9	-1.1%
HIgherEducation	$2,583.9	$2,738.7	5.7%	$2,743.5	0.2%
Corrections	$2,098.7	$2,179.2	3.7%	$2,258.0	3.5%
GeneralGovernment	$2,182.7	$2,381.2	8.3%	$2,387.8	0.3%
GRFProgramTotal	**$34,187.3**	**$35,173.6**	**2.8%**	**$39,090.0**	**10.0%**

State and local partnership

In our state the Legislature advances the concept that the funding of our schools should be primarily a state and local partnership. The degree of financial support by the 3 major levels of government; local, state and federal, is given below:

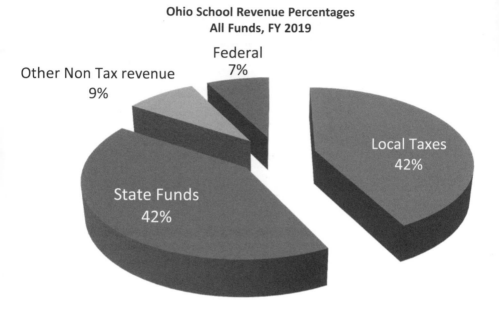

Ohio School Revenue Percentages
All Funds, FY 2019

Federal
7%

Other Non Tax revenue
9%

Local Taxes
42%

State Funds
42%

Public School Operating Revenue by Source.

Public schools have many sources of revenue. Local property taxes, the majority of which are voted on in most Ohio districts, are the mainstay of school funding. The various general categories of state aid follow. Federal aid, mostly targeted to support specific functions is next. See the chart below for the breakdown, provided by the Ohio Legislative Service Commission.

Public School Operating Revenues by Source, Typical		
Source Components	Revenue (in millions)	Percentage of Source
State Sources		
Foundation aid formula	$ 8,248.9	82.7%
Property tax rollbacks	$ 1,163.2	11.7%
TPP direct reimbursements	$ 181.8	1.8%
Preschool special education	$ 115.5	1.2%
Casino tax	$ 92.0	1.0%
Directly funded scholarships	$ 61.2	0.6%
Special education transportation	$ 56.3	0.6%
Payments for funding ESC support services	$ 43.8	0.4%
Community school facilities	$ 16.6	0.2%
Total State Sources	$ 9,979.2	100.0%
Local Sources		
Property taxes	$ 8,934.6	95.3%
Income taxes	$ 444.1	4.7%
Total State Sources	$ 9,378.7	100.0%
Federal Sources		
ESEA Title 1	$ 537.5	48.7%
Special education (IDEA)	$ 424.5	38.5%
Improving teacher quality	$ 71.8	6.5%
Career-technical education	$ 35.9	3.3%
Preschool special education	$ 10.6	1.0%
English language acquisition	$ 10.1	0.9%
Student support and academic enrichment	$ 7.2	0.7%
Rural education	$ 3.3	0.3%
Homeless children education	$ 2.1	0.2%
Total Federal Sources	$ 1,102.9	100.0%
Total all sources	$ 20,460.8	

Data courtesy Ohio Legislative Service Commission

Educated Voters are Needed

This unique feature about public support of education in Ohio is not that this support requires huge sums of money, but that so large a portion of it is subject to a direct vote of the people. Every vote requires a decision. Every decision should be based upon facts and adequate information. This basic principle is the foundation of the democratic process where decision-making power is exercised through a free vote of the people. This book will help the reader understand the financial workings of Ohio public schools.

Important Concepts
of Local School Finance

In the whole area of Ohio school finance, the concepts of local
school finance may be of greatest interest to you. This is true because
the major share of the local money provided for schools must be voted
on by the local citizens. In addition, this source of taxation for schools
affects every local resident who lives in a private home or apartment
building, or who owns business property in the school district.

Given below is the local school finance picture, with terms and
explanations of how each of the areas operates at the local level.

A warning here is that the local school finance structure has a
number of related parts. Some must be referred to in explaining others.
All cannot be explained at the same time. Although an attempt has been
made to place the elements in an understandable sequence, the reader
may have to double back to previous sections in a number of cases, with
knowledge gained later on in the chapter, in order to gain a good understanding of each element.

Cost per pupil

The amount of money which a school district spends in a school
year divided by the number of students enrolled in the schools during
that year equals the cost per pupil.

$$\frac{\text{Yearly school expenditures}}{\text{Yearly school enrollment}} = \text{cost per pupil}$$

If a school district had a yearly budget expenditure of $20
million and a school enrollment of 2,000 students, its cost per pupil
would be $10,000.

$$\frac{\$20,000,000 \text{ expenditures}}{2,000 \text{ pupils enrolled}} = \$10,000 \text{ cost per pupil}$$

Since many of the factors which contribute to a good school
system cost money, cost per pupil is one of the best measures of educational quality.

Valuation per pupil

The assessed value of all property located within a school district which is taxed for school purposes, divided by the number of pupils enrolled in the school, equals the valuation per pupil.

$$\frac{\text{total school-taxed property in district}}{\text{school enrollment}} = \text{valuation per pupil}$$

If a school district levied taxes upon $300 million worth of property located within its boundaries and had 3,000 pupils enrolled in the schools, the valuation per pupil would be $100,000.

$$\frac{\$300,000,000 \text{ total assessed valuation}}{3,000 \text{ pupils enrolled}} = \$100,000 \text{ valuation per pupil}$$

The tax valuation per pupil is the best measure of taxable wealth available to support a school district's educational program. The more taxable property there is per student, the greater the income which can be produced through a specific local tax rate to educate that student.

Property tax

A major share of all financial support for local school districts is raised by taxing property located within the district. The property tax takes the following forms:

The general property tax is levied upon land and buildings located within the school district. It is essentially a real estate or real property tax. Every owner of private and business property in the district, including public utilities, pays this tax. The tax is divided into Class 1 (Residential and Agricultural) and Class 2 (All other). Property owned by governmental, charitable and religious institutions used in the conduct of their business is exempt from taxation.

REAL PROPERTY

Class 1	Class 2
Residential and Agricultural	All other (Commercial and industrial)

The tax rate

This rate shows, in number of mills, the taxes assessed against your property by the various governmental entities which have the authority to levy, or ask the voters to approve through a referendum, property taxes against your property. There are over 4,000 taxing jurisdictions in Ohio, each with its own tax rate. The tax rate for schools, for example, may be 30 mills. The county, city, library or other government authorities may also be levying a tax against your home, each having a different tax rate. Your total property tax rate may be 45 mills.

The county treasurer may have available a sheet showing the tax rate levied by each taxing entity and a total tax rate for each taxing district.

Mills

Local tax rates against property are always computed in mills. Additional school levies are presented in mills. Despite its wide use, few citizens know that a mill is one-tenth of a penny.

One Mill is 1/10 of One Penny

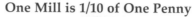

One Cent

A little multiplication will produce the following information about a mill:
• A mill produces $1.00 in tax income for every $1,000 of assessed value of property it is levied against.
• A mill produces $1,000 in tax income for every $1 million of assessed value of property it is levied against.

If the total property assessed valuation for tax purposes in your school district was $50 million and the district had an effective tax rate of 30 mills, the income produced for schools would be $1,500,000 per year.

Types of mills

Although a mill is one-tenth of a cent in all cases, there are three categories of mills which affect school districts.

Inside Mills – local governments, by statute, may levy up to 10 mills in taxes without a vote of the people. The mills are divided up between schools, municipalities and other agencies of government, with schools typically receiving between four to six mills as their share. These mills are called "inside" mills because they are inside the 10-mill statutory limitation and were levied without a vote of the people.

Outside Mills or Voted Mills - This includes all mills approved by a vote of the people. A school district with 30 mills levied for operation may have, for example, five "inside" mills and 25 voted mills.

Effective Mills - As a result of HB 920, when a reassessment or update of property values takes place and the value of real property has increased due to inflation, a tax credit factor is applied to the voted mills. This prevents an increase in the tax bill of the property owner because inflation has increased the value of the property. The effect of the tax credit is that less than 100% of the voted mills are applied to the new and increased value of the property. The mills actually collected are called *effective mills*. District taxpayers may have *voted* 40 mills for their schools, but only 30 *effective mills* are being collected.

Property tax capacity

There is a wide difference in the amount of property per pupil subject to school taxes in Ohio districts. Property values per pupil in tax year (TY) 2019 (latest available) ranged from $76,141 for the first quintile and $242,090 for the fifth quintile. The same one mill school tax will raise $76 per pupil in a district with $76,000 of property value per pupil and $242 per pupil for a district with a per pupil value of $242,000. The statewide medium was $145,000 per pupil.

This factor, property tax capacity, explains why there is such a large difference in local income per pupil in Ohio districts. A district with $242 available per pupil per mill has a lot better opportunity to provide a quality education for its students than one with only $76 available per pupil per mill.

A major aim of state aid to schools is to level out this difference to the extent possible, giving more state money to districts with lower property tax capacity and less to districts with higher capacity.

Property tax effort

The basic equation that determines school income at the local level is mills applied against taxable property. The state can help to mitigate the variation of local property value but the mills factor, the willingness of citizens to tax themselves to support their local schools, is an individual school district matter. The state does require a minimum local tax rate for schools of 20 mills in order to receive any state aid. All Ohio districts meet that minimum requirement. The citizens in some will not vote for a higher rate.

In a Typical Tax year there will be over 200 districts at the 20 mill floor. The statewide median rate is about 40 mills. The Shaker Heights City School District is the poster child for local support of their school district with an effective tax rate of 91.81 mills in tax year 2020.

One can see that the wide disparities in income which low wealth districts contend with are attributable to both the low tax base and willingness of local citizens to tax themselves for the support of their local schools.

Sale value, assessed value, reappraisals

The property tax is an ad valorem tax, which means, "in proportion to the value." Once we have decided to tax according to the value of property, we must then uniformly apply some system to determine the value of property, to assess its value.

What a home, or any other real property, will sell for in the open market, assuming a willing buyer and a willing seller with neither being under any pressure to buy or sell and both having knowledge of all relevant facts, is known as true value, market value, or sale value. This is commonly referred to as an "arms length" sale.

The county auditor in each of Ohio's 88 counties has the task of appraising all taxable real property in the county to determine its value.

While additional construction will be appraised as it comes on the tax duplicate, once every six years the auditor must conduct a complete reappraisal (revaluation) of all taxable real property in the county. Once every three years a form of reappraisal, called an "update," is also conducted.

The auditor generally hires a firm specializing in this field to do the reappraisals. A representative of this firm will make an on-site inspection of all real property. The inspection is done according to a detailed set of rules and is very thorough. Following this inspection, the appraiser makes an estimate of the sale value of the property, which the appraiser refers to as its "true value in money."

However, when local taxes are levied against property in your school district, sale value or "true value in money" is not used. Instead, a percentage of this value is used, called the assessment rate. After the sale value is multiplied by the assessment rate, then we have the assessed value, which is the value set for tax purposes.

The Ohio Supreme Court has declared that the same assessment rate must apply to all real property (land and structures thereon) throughout the state which is subject to property taxation. The Board of Tax Appeals has adopted a rule requiring that the assessed value be 35% of sale value.

Thus, if your property has a market value of $100,000 and is assessed for tax purposes at 35% of market value, your property will go on the tax lists with an assessed value of $35,000 ($100,000 x 35% = $35,000).

10

You would pay taxes on only $35,000 worth of property even though you could sell that property for $100,000.

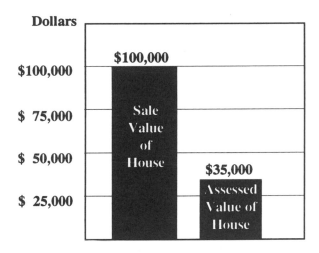

Your county auditor, in his or her office, has listed the assessed value of all parcels of property in your county. This information is available to the public.

YEAR OF SEXENNIAL REAPPRAISAL AND TRIENNIAL UPDATE FOR OHIO'S 88 COUNTIES 2020-2025

2020 REAPPRAISAL COUNTIES	2021 REAPPRAISAL COUNTIES	2022 REAPPRAISAL COUNTIES	2023 REAPPRAISAL COUNTIES	2024 REAPPRAISAL COUNTIES	2025 REAPPRAISAL COUNTIES
ASHLAND	ALLEN	ADAMS	AUGLAIZE	BELMONT	CARROLL
ASHTABULA	COSHOCTON	COLUMBIANA	CLINTON	BROWN	CHAMPION
ATHENS	GUERNSEY	HANCOCK	DARKE	CRAWFORD	CLARK
BUTLER	SANDUSKY	HOCKING	DEFIANCE	CUYAHOGA	FAIRFIELD
CLERMONT	VINTON	HOLMES	DELAWARE	ERIE HIGHLAND	LOGAN
FULTON		LAWRENCE	FRANKLIN	HURON	MARION
GREENE		MEIGS	GALLIA	JEFFERSON	MEDINA
KNOX		MONROE	GEAUGA	LAKE	MIAMI
MADISON		PAULDING	HAMILTON	LORAIN	ROSS
MONTGOMERY		SCIOTO	HARDIN	LUCAS	UNION
NOBLE		TUSCARAWAS	HARRISON	MORGAN	WYANDOT
SUMMIT		WASHINGTON	HENRY	MUSKINGUM	
WAYNE			JACKSON	OTTAWA	
			LICKING	PORTAGE	
			MAHONING	STARK	
			MERCER	WARREN	
			MORROW	WILLIAMS	
			PERRY		
			PICKAWAY		
			PIKE		
			PREBLE		
			PUTNAM		
			RICHLAND		
			SENECA		
			SHELBY		
			TRUMBULL		
			VAN WERT		
			WOOD		

2021 UPDATE COUNTIES
BELMONT, BROWN, CRAWFORD, CUYAHOGA, ERIE, FAYETTE, HIGHLAND, HURON, JEFFERSON, LAKE, LORAIN, LUCAS, MORGAN, MUSKINGUM, OTTAWA, PORTAGE, STARK, WARREN, WILLIAMS

2020 UPDATE COUNTIES
AUGLAIZE, CLINTON, DARKE, DEFIANCE, DELAWARE, FRANKLIN, GALLIA, GEAUGA, HAMILTON, HARDIN, HARRISON, HENRY, JACKSON, LICKING, MAHONING, MERCER, MORROW, PERRY, PICKAWAY, PIKE, PREBLE, PUTNAM, RICHLAND, SENECA, SHELBY, TRUMBULL, VAN WERT, WOOD

2022 UPDATE COUNTIES
CARROLL, CHAMPION, CLARK, FAIRFIELD, LOGAN, MARION, MEDINA, MIAMI, ROSS, UNION, WYANDOT

2023 UPDATE COUNTIES
ASHLAND, ASHTABULA, ATHENS, BUTLER, CLERMONT, FULTON, GREENE, KNOX, MADISON, MONTGOMERY, NOBLE, SUMMIT, WAYNE

2024 UPDATE COUNTIES
ALLEN, COSHOCTON, GUERNSEY, SANDUSKY, VINTON

2025 UPDATE COUNTIES
ADAMS, COLUMBIANA, HANCOCK, HOCKING, HOLMES, LAWRENCE, MEIGS, MONROE, PAULDING, SCIOTO, TUSCARAWAS, WASHINGTON

Note: Updates take place 3 years after each reappraisal

Challenges to Assessed Value

The real property assessment process, which determines your property tax bill, is as exact as smart people can make it. However, mistakes occur. These errors are likely due to the number of people doing the reassessment and the huge volume of properties which must be assessed. There are over 500,000 properties in Cuyahoga County alone. Similar numbers will be found in other urban counties.

12

There are times when properties sell for much more than the last assessment indicated they were worth. The sale value of property is considered prima face evidence of its worth; proof enough on its face. A new owner cannot simply claim that he or she paid more for the property than it was really worth and thereby should be taxed as though the property was worth less than he or she just paid for it. School districts can immediately challenge these assessments, after a sale value is established, and get the property tax revised upward based on the new value. Beware, however, the political fallout if the revisions apply to residential property sales.

On the other hand, property owners may feel that the Auditor has overvalued their property. They seek to establish a new, and lower, value and gain a tax reduction. The first opportunity is by participating in an <u>informal hearing</u> with the County's appraiser. If not satisfied there, in each county there is a board designated to hear appeals to assessed value. It maybe be called a <u>Board of Revision</u> or a <u>Board of Tax Revision</u>. According to a schedule established by that board, any person, can appeal for a <u>reduction</u> in its assessed value. Most of these appeals take place shortly after a county reassessment of update. Experience has shown that 1% to 2% of property owner's appeal for a reduction.

The final step is to the <u>Ohio Board of Tax Appeals</u>. In the appeals process, the value which the Auditor gave to the property is presumed to be correct. The burden of proof is on the property owner, who has to submit credible evidence that the Auditor overvalued the property. Evidence could be pictures of the poor condition of the inside of the home, which the Auditor did not inspect. It could be recent true arms length sale price for less than the Auditor's value or the lower appraised value of comparable homes located within the area. Though this seems a daunting task, in Cuyahoga County, Ohio's largest, approximately 70-75% of the homeowners and 50% of the businesses which file for reductions are granted all or part of the reduction requested.

Using the same procedure as outlined above, any individual or school district can file for an increase in the taxable value of any piece of property in the county. The Auditor lists the sale and assessed values of all properties sold. If the sale price shows that any property is underassessed, and appeal can be filed for an increase in the assessed value, using the sale price as proof of the real value.

Property sale prices in forced transactions, such as sheriff's sales, foreclosures, short sales or bank owned property sales are not considered "arms length" transactions and are not included in the calculations when the Auditor determines property values. These sales do not involve "a willing buyer and a willing seller," although these types of sales have driven property values down.

Appraisers do point out that properties such as these may have been vandalized or not cared for properly and should not be considered normal transactions.

State Issue #1 and House Bill 920

HB 920, often credited to the leading role in its promotion and passage played by then Cuyahoga County Auditor, then Governor, now retired Senator George Voinovich, intended to eliminate unvoted property tax increases. Prior to HB 920, if a reassessment or update showed that property had increased in value by 20%, the tax bill on that property would also increase by 20%; thus an unvoted property tax increase. HB 920 eliminated the property tax on the increase in property value caused by inflation. We will see specifically how it works in a later section.

The value of residential property increased sharply in the 1970's, while the value of industrial, commercial and public utility real property had shown a much more modest increase. Since reassessment and updates are designed to catch these changes in value and reflect them in the taxes paid, home and farm owners had been paying higher taxes as the value of their property increased RELATIVE TO THE TOTAL TAX DUPLICATE, while owners of other types of real property had paid only small increases and, in some cases, actually enjoyed a cut in property taxes following a reassessment. Because unvoted property tax increases usually produce a voter outcry, and because the General Assembly is sensitive to voter dissatisfaction, the legislature in Ohio has a history of responding to taxpayer complaints with legislation designed to alleviate their perceived financial distress. House Bill 920 was in itself such a measure.

Selective inflation, combined with House Bill 920, shifted what was judged to be an unfair tax burden on to home and farm owners. Thus, in 1980, a constitutional amendment, State Issue #1, was placed on the ballot by the Legislature and approved by the voters in November of that year. It established two separate classes of real property. Agricultural and residential property is now in a separate class with all other real property in a different class.

Now the tax reduction factor (tax credit) is applied separately to the two classes of property, rather than to the total tax duplicate.

In general, House Bill 920 and State Issue #1 have the following effect upon tax bills following reappraisals or readjustments in the assessed value of property:

• If your property increases in value the same percentage as the average increase of all real property in your classification in the taxing district, your tax bill for voted millage will not change.

• If your property increases in value more than the average increase of

all real property in your classification in the taxing district, your tax bill for voted millage will increase.
• If your property increases less than the average increase of all real property in your classification in the taxing district, your tax bill for voted millage will decrease.

Tax credits

House Bill 920 first introduced the concept of real property tax credits *(throughout this booklet tax credit and tax reduction will have the same meaning)* to Ohio. It was enacted as a result of protests from citizens who were being served markedly higher tax bills following reappraisals. The higher bills came as a result of a rapid increase in the worth of real property, especially homes, when compared to other classes of taxable property. This resulted in a shift in the tax burden from business and public utilities to the homeowners.

House Bill 920 further mandated:
• that reappraisals be continued on a sexennial (six-year) basis.
• that the Commissioner of Tax Equalization may order a readjustment in the assessed value of property in all counties in the third year following reappraisal. This is commonly called an update.
• that real property owners be given a tax credit (reduction) equal to any increase in the value of all real property in the taxing district as a result of inflation as shown in reappraisals or readjustments. This tax credit does not apply to other types of taxable property, nor to unvoted inside millage.

The legislation provides that the assessed value of property will not be changed more than once every three years, and that the property tax bill of the average homeowner for voted millage will not be increas-ed as a result of inflation as shown by reappraisals or readjustments.

The tax credit works like this:
Assume your home has a sale value of $100,000 and is assessed at 35% of that, for tax purposes, or $35,000. The voted millage in your school district is 25 mills. Your tax bill as a result of voted mills is $875. ($35,000 x 25 mills = $875)

A reappraisal of update shows the assessed value of your home has been increased from $35,000 to $40,000, the result of inflation. This is an increase of $5,000 or 14.3%. You might expect your voted school tax bill to increase by 14.3%, but that will not be the case.

Assume all real property in your taxing district is assessed at $30,000,000 and, with a voted tax rate of 25 mills, produces $750,000 in revenue. As a result of reappraisal or readjustment the value of all real property is increased to $35,000,000, an increase of 16.7%.

Now the question is, if we keep the voted mills the same, what kind of tax reduction factor would we have to use to prevent the revenue for schools and the average tax bill from increasing?

Find this number by dividing the old assessed value by the new assessed value, getting an answer of 85.7%. The average real property owner would be required to pay only 85.7% of the voted mills. $35,000,000 assessed value x (25 voted mills x 85.7% = 21.43 effective mills) = $750,000 for the schools, the same amount as the schools received before the reassessment.

Applying this tax credit to your property produces the following tax bill - $40,000 assessed home value x (25 mills x 85.7% = 21.43 effective mills) = $857 yearly tax bill to the schools.

In this situation, your tax bill on voted mills would actually be reduced from $875 to $857 even though your property increased in value. The tax reduction takes place because the increase in value of your property was less than the average increase for residential and agricultural real property in your taxing district as a whole.

Be aware, however that your total tax bill may increase as a result of inside or unvoted millage being applied to the higher property values and by newly voted tax levies. All agencies of government which tax property, including schools, municipalities, counties, libraries or other agencies, affect your property tax bill. An agency, besides your school district, may have passed a levy which is being added to your tax bill.

10% and 2.5% millage rollbacks

In addition to the tax credits granted to Ohio citizens as part of HB 920, for a number of years a 10% property tax rollback has been in effect. The state pays the equivalent of 10% of your local millage to the school district, further reducing your tax bill. HB 66, passed in 2005, eliminated the rollback for certain real property used in business but maintained the rollback for residential and agricultural property.

House Bill 204, enacted in 1979, increased the rollback to 12.5% for owner-occupied homesteads 2nd one surrounding acre only.

One of the most significant parts of HB 59 was the repeal of these two tax- credits for new and replacement levies, starting with the November of 2013 election. Now local taxpayers will have to pay 12.5% more for each new levy passed, which may lead to a lower passage rate for these school issues.

Homestead exemption

A common complaint among senior adults when there is a school issue on the ballot is, "I live on a fixed income. I am getting taxed out of my home."

In an attempt to help this large voting bloc, as well as public schools,

16

a great deal of legislative attention has been devoted to this issue. In 1970, Ohio voters approved a constitutional amendment, permitting a homestead exemption that reduced property taxes for lower income senior citizens. The program has taken different permutations over the years. The exemption, which takes the form of a credit on property tax bills, allows qualifying homeowners to exempt up to $25,000 of the market value of their dwelling, plus up to one acre of land, from all local property taxes. A homestead with a market value of $100,000 would be taxed as having a market value of $75,000.

The homestead exemption is now means tested for individuals who turn 65 in 2014 and all following years. Older residents already receiving the credit are grandfathered in. The amount is adjusted for inflation each year. In 2017, the income threshold is $31,800, based on the Ohio Adjusted Gross Income (line 3) of the tax return.

Eligible residents must:

*Qualify under the means test

*Be at least 65 or turn 65 in the year for which they apply

*Be totally and permanently disabled as of January 1 of the year for which they apply

*Be the surviving spouse of a person who was receiving the exemption at the time of death, and was at least 59 years old at the time of death.

Application for the exemption is made by filing a form with the County Auditor in the county in which the applicant resides. Once approved, the deduction is in force as long as the applicant lives in the homestead for which the approval was granted.

There is no tax loss to the local school district. The state will reimburse the school district for money lost due to the homestead exemption.

*Source: Ohio Department of Taxation

Your property tax bill

It is the task of each county treasurer to put all these factors together, compute your tax bill and present you with a detailed accounting.

Primary Owner
Property Address
Tax Mailing Address
Legal Description
Property Class   SINGLE FAMILY DWELLING
Parcel Number   862-20-001
Taxset   Mayfield Hts.
Tax Year   2020

Assessed Values		Market Values		Flags	
Land Value	$18,200	Land Value	$52,000	Owner Occupancy Credit	N
Building Value	$38,220	Building Value	$109,200	Homestead Reduction	N
Total Value	$56,420	Total Value	$161,200	Foreclosure	N
Homestead Value	$			Cert. Pending	N
				Cert. Sold	N
Half Year Charge Amounts		Rates		Payment Plan	N
Gross Tax	$3,577.03	Full Rate	126.80		
Less 920 Reduction	$1,182.12	920 Reduction Rate	.330476		
Sub Total	$2,394.91	Effective Rate	84.895682	Escrow	
10% Reduction Amount	$198.18			Escrow	N
Owner Occupancy Credit	$.00			Payment Amount	$.00
Homestead Reduction Amount	$.00				
Total Assessments	$125.00				
Half Year Net Taxes	$2,321.73				

	Charges	Payments	Balance Due
Tax Balance Summary	$4,643.46	$4,643.46	$.00

2020 (pay in 2021) Charge and Payment Detail

Taxset
Mayfield Hts.

	Charge Type	Charges	Payments	Balance Due
	1st half tax	$2,196.73	$2,196.73	$.00
	1ST HALF BALANCE	$2,196.73	$2,196.73	$.00
	2nd half tax	$2,196.73	$2,196.73	$.00
	2ND HALF BALANCE	$2,196.73	$2,196.73	$.00
C100410A-Sewer Maintenance				
	1st half tax	$125.00	$125.00	$.00
	1ST HALF BALANCE	$125.00	$125.00	$.00
	2nd half tax	$125.00	$125.00	$.00
	2ND HALF BALANCE	$125.00	$125.00	$.00
		Charges	Payments	Balance Due
Total Balance		$4,643.46	$4,643.46	$.00

* Taxes are updated within the hour

HB 920 - *negative impact on schools*

Although HB 920 had a number of provisions, the effect of the bill on school funding has been devastating. Stated simply, ONCE A SCHOOL LEVY IS PASSED IN YOUR LOCAL DISTRICT, THE AMOUNT OF MONEY WHICH YOUR SCHOOL DISTRICT CAN

RECEIVE FROM THAT SCHOOL LEVY APPLIED AGAINST THE TAX DUPLICATE WHICH EXISTED WHEN THE ISSUE WAS PASSED CAN NEVER INCREASE. When reassessment and updates show that inflation has increased the value of property, a tax credit is applied to make certain that schools receive no more income from the voted mills applied against that property. Schools also receive a second hit related to HB 920, called "Phantom Revenue," discussed in a later chapter.

See the illustration to understand how the HB 920 process works.

Home Sale Value	Assessed Value 35%		Voted Mills		School Income
$80,000	$28,000	X	40	=	$1,120

After Reassessment. . .

Home Sale Value Up 10%	Assessed Value 35%		Effective Mills		School Income
$88,000	$30,800	X	40.00 mills −3.64 mills 36.36 mills	=	$1,120

Note that 40 mills were approved by the voters. Because of HB 920, 36.36 mills are actually being collected.

See the chart below to understand the cumulative impact of voted and effective mills.

Total Tax Approved vs. Tax Collected
Sample School District

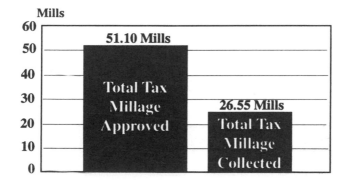

Thus we have the concept of VOTED MILLS and EFFECTIVE MILLS. Voted mills are those mills which the taxpayers have approved. Effective mills are the mills actually collected.

Please see the "Raising Funds for Schools at the Local Level" chapter of this book to see how the Legislature has enabled districts to pass *Conversion Levies,* an attempt to at least partially alleviate the negative effects of HB 920 for district which are eligible for and can pass this type of levy.

Computing the cost of a tax increase

1. Determine the assessed value of the property to be taxed, in thousands of dollars.
2. Multiply the millage rate by the figure produced in Step 1.

Let's take an example. District A is asking its citizens to approve an additional school levy of five mills. You own property in the district which has a sale value of $100,000. What will the levy cost you if passed?

To put all this together in a basic formula, calculation of property taxes has only two elements:

> **Taxable Value X Property Tax Rate = Property Taxes Levied**

The calculation becomes more complex because of the issues described in previous pages. **Types of mills** (inside and voted), **tax reduction factors** after reappraisals and updates which produce an **effective tax rate** and a **tax credit** (homestead exemption) are all factored in to the final tax bill. A more complete formula is:

> **Property Taxes Levied - impact of tax reduction factors =**
>
> **Taxes Charged - credits = Net property Taxes.**

Now that you have the basic system, you can compute the cost of any basic levy for additional operating expenses by using the following method:

Step 1. Determine the assessed value of your property in thousands of dollars.

Assessed value is 35% of market value.
$100,000   market value of property
  x 35%   assessment rate
$ 35,000   assessed value for tax purposes
The answer in thousands of dollars is 35.

Step 2. Multiply the millage rate by the figure produced in Step 1.

$$\begin{array}{r} 35 \\ \times\,5 \\ \hline \$175.00 \end{array} \begin{array}{l} \text{assessed value in thousands of dollars} \\ \text{millage increase being requested} \\ \text{cost of levy to you per year}\, . \end{array}$$

(The tax will be less if you receive a homestead exemption).

Typically each school district will accurately compute the annual cost of a proposed school tax issue for a range of home values in the school district, including the average home, and publish this information through local news stories and in campaign literature.

Some newspapers, such as the Cleveland Plain Dealer, will calculate the cost of a proposed tax increase for you on line. This is a particular benefit as they can use their resources to calculate the cost of issues such as conversion levies or combined issues which are more complex than simple millage additional levies, the example of which is given in this book. You provide the name of your school district and the value of your home and they do the rest. See below for the actual CPD calculation of a proposed 6.75 mill added levy for the Amherst Exempted Village Schools in Lorain County:

School District *	Amherst	▼
House Value (thousands) *	100 000	
(Type 100 for $100,000, 200 for $200,000, etc. up to 1,000 for $1 million)		
	Search	

Created with Caspio

Amherst

6.75-mill tax request
Taxes shown here are based a home
with market value of $100,000.

*Total annual bill for current school taxes	$1,005.32
Increase if tax passes	$206.72
Percent change	21%
This is a new tax request	

* Note: Actual annual tax bills are higher because they also include taxes for cities, libraries, parks, the county and other taxing bodies.

Created with Caspio

Your house payment and taxes

If you have a mortgage on your home, the mortgage company or bank will offer to serve as the agent for paying your property taxes and home insurance. They will set your monthly payment at an amount sufficient to pay the principal and interest on your loan, plus the amount necessary to pay your taxes and insurance. These latter amounts are placed in an escrow account, earning interest for the mortgage holder, until the bills come due for payment.

Since the property tax bill is typically sent to the mortgage holder, the homeowner does not see the tax bill.

If any of the elements which make up your monthly mortgage payment change during the year, your mortgage payment will change. You receive a notification of the change, probably with minimum explanation.

Many is the homeowner who travels a long odyssey trying to find out specifically why the mortgage payment has increased. The suspicion is that there is a tax increase in there somewhere, but who gets the additional money?

Here is one thing on which you can be clear: If your mortgage payment has increased and the voters of your school district have not passed a school tax increase of some kind, the schools did not get the additional money. The only exception is the small amount they may receive from inside millage when there is a reassessment or an update.

If the increase in your monthly mortgage payment was due to a property tax increase, the money may have gone to the municipality, the county, the library or other taxing authority, or any combination of the above. There are 3,392 taxing authorities in Ohio.

All of these taxing authorities, and the schools, operate under different rules. As an example, cities can levy up to 10 mills, called charter millage, which is not subject to House Bill 920.

The taxes produced by city charter millage do increase in proportion to any increase in the value of your property when a reassessment or update takes place. This fact alone helps explain why schools, whose major source of income is frozen, are on the ballot so frequently while other taxing authorities are not.

Raising Funds for Schools at the Local Level

Levies, bond issues - What's the difference?

Boards of education may present three different kinds of property tax issues to their voters - operating levies, permanent improvement levies and bond issues. It is important for the reader to understand the distinctions between these issues since there is a common misunderstanding that they are one and the same.

Operating levies

An operating levy is a tax, the proceeds from which can be used for any legal expenditure by a board of education. The great bulk of funds derived from operating levies are used to pay the day-by-day operating costs of running a school district - salaries for personnel; purchase of books, supplies and equipment; repair of buildings and equipment; and other like costs. Also, operating levy proceeds can be used for building construction, for permanent improvements such as sidewalks and parking lots, for the purchase of furniture and equipment including buses and for any other expenditure not forbidden by law.

Permanent improvement levies

A permanent improvement (PI) levy is a tax, the proceeds from which can only be used to construct, add to or repair buildings, lay sidewalks, build parking lots and make many other such improvements of school property and assets. Permanent improvements are generally considered to be items lasting five years or more. Permanent improvement levies for specific projects can be voted for a maximum of five years. Levies for general, on-going permanent improvements may be levied for a continuing period of time. Proceeds from permanent improvement levies cannot be used to pay current operating costs.

"Continuing period of time" means that the levy has no expiration date. It continues unless the residents of the school district later vote to reduce or eliminate it. *Ohio Revised Code sections 5705.21 and 5705.25.*

County sales tax for permanent improvements

It is now possible for school districts, through the County Commissioners, to place a county wide sales tax of up to one half of one percent (0.5%) on the ballot to provide permanent improvements for schools. The tax can be for a limited or continuing period of time.

The County Commissioners of a county agreeing to place such an issue on the ballot must first create a nine member Community Improvements Board (ORC 307.283) and recommend guidelines for its operation. The CIB develops the guidelines for the distribution of taxes once collected. Its members determine how the income raised will be allocated. This process is done through grant applications.

The allocation plan is negotiable and may differ from county to county. In all three of the counties which have attempted to pass such a tax, the plan adopted involved distributing the income collected on a per pupil basis to districts or schools educating students who are residents within the county. This included the distribution of funds to the county's career center.

The first county to successfully use this new taxing authority was Medina County, which passed a one half percent (0.5%) sales tax earmarked specifically for school improvements on May 8 of 2007. This tax was levied for 30 years.

The districts which have attempted to pass the county income tax have advanced several selling points for the tax, among them: (1) It is not another property tax. Future permanent improvement needs may be met by this tax rather than a property tax. (2) It is a tax levied at the point of sale which means that part of the revenue raised could be paid by shoppers who do not live within the county. (3) It is a pay-as-you-go tax. (4) Income will grow with inflation. (5) This tax is not subject to HB 920. (6) It is fairer to people on fixed incomes as the tax paid is dependent on the amount spent.

Passing this kind of tax requires the highest skill in political consensus building. The leaders of the participating school districts must agree, then a majority of the county commissioners, then the Community Improvements Board, then the voters. ORC 5739.026(A)(4), 5741.023

Bond issues

A bond issue is a tax, the proceeds from which can only be used to retire bonds or notes issued by boards of education to raise funds to pay the direct and related costs of permanent improvements. In general, bond issues are voted to pay the cost of school construction and major renovations. The items for which these funds can be used are stated on the ballot when the issue is presented to the people. Money can be spent only for these authorized purposes. (See next chapter).

Proceeds from bond issues cannot be used to pay the day-by-day operating expenses of a school district.

The misunderstanding concerning the purpose of these different kinds of taxes commonly occurs after citizens of a school district pass a bond issue to build a new school. A year or so later, after the school is built and ready to use, the board of education may come back to the voters for an operating levy in order to raise funds to operate the new school. At this point many citizens will remember voting for the bond issue and wonder why the proceeds from this tax cannot be used to operate the school. The answer is that this procedure would be illegal. Proceeds from the bond issue can only be used to pay for the building program itself. This may also include the purchase of land, furniture, architect fees, etc. There is usually no money left after the building program is completed.

Think of these three categories of income as being like water running downhill. The funds can only flow in one direction. Operating levy income can be used for operations, permanent improvements and major building projects. Some districts, notably Perry Local in Lake County, have built schools and paid for them with operating funds. PI levy income can be used for permanent improvements and major building projects, but cannot be used to pay for general operations, including salaries for staff. Bond issue proceeds can only be used for the major building items listed on the ballot, not for minor permanent improvements or general operations.

General Fund

PI Fund

Bond Issue Fund

Types of operating levies

Under current law boards of education may place different kinds of operating levies before their voters, as follows:

Regular operating levy for current expenses

In this kind of levy, a millage rate is submitted to the voters for approval, not a dollar amount. For example, the rate may be six mills or seven mills. This levy can be voted for from one to five years or can be voted for a continuing period of time. *Ohio revised code sections 3501.01, 5748.02, 5705.19, 5705.194, 5705.21*

Emergency levy

This type of levy is submitted to the electorate as a dollar amount. For example, "The emergency levy will raise $1,000,000 per year." A millage amount will appear on the ballot, but this amount is advisory only. The mills are adjusted each year of the levy to account for changes in the tax duplicate in order to keep the school income constant for the term of the levy. An emergency levy can be voted for a period of time from one to five years. After the voted period of time has elapsed, the levy expires, unless the voters vote to renew it. *Ohio Revised Code sections 5705.194 through 5705.197.*

Millage incremental tax levy

This type of levy, which can be voted for a continuing period of time or from one to 10 years, is for current expenses. It is voted in mills. The difference here is that a school district can ask the voters to approve up to five different millage rates to be levied in specified years. For example, the voters may be asked to approve a five mill tax increase in 2009, an additional two mills in 2010, an additional two mills in 2011, and an additional two increases until the levy expires. *Ohio Revised Code Section 5705.212.*

Dollar incremental tax levy

This type of levy, which can be voted from one to 10 years, is for current expenses. It is expressed not in mills, but in dollar amounts or percentage increases. As with millage incremental tax levies, up to five different dollar amounts or percentage increases may be submitted for voter approval, to be first levied in specified years. For example, a dollar incremental tax levy could be a tax to produce an additional $1,000,000 in 2009, an additional $750,000 in 2010 and an additional $500,000 in 2011 and two more increases until the levy expires. *Ohio Revised Code Section 5705.213.*

Replacement levy

Senate Bill 257 became effective in 1990. The bill authorizes several political subdivisions - including city, local, exempted village districts and county school financing districts - to submit replacement levies (as opposed to renewal levies) for voter approval when an existing levy is expiring. A replacement levy can replace all or a portion of an expiring levy. It must have the same purpose as an expiring levy.

Under Senate Bill 257, school districts may propose replacement levies for current expenses, permanent improvements, or school district public library expenses. *Ohio Revised Code Section 5705.192.*

A replacement levy approved by the voters can raise more revenue than the levy it replaces, although both appear to levy the same millage rate. The reason is that the original levy which is being replaced may have been through one or more reassessment and updates, depending upon how long ago the original levy was passed. With each reassessment and update, if the value of real property in the school district has increased due to inflation, a HB 920 tax credit factor will have been applied to the voted levy. It may have been voted for 6 mills originally. Years later, because of HB 920, only 3 effective mills are being collected because the value of the property the original issue was levied against has doubled in value due to inflation.

A replacement levy may be for the same 6 mills as was originally voted. However, the replacement levy for 6 mills will actually be replacing a levy which has now been reduced to 3 effective mills. If the replacement levy passes, there will be a 3 mill tax increase.

A replacement levy must be proposed by a two-thirds vote of the entire school board. It must be called a replacement levy on the ballot, must appear separately on the ballot, and cannot be joined with the renewal or replacement of any other existing levy.

Combination or dual purpose issues

In 1997 Boards of Education were given authority by the Legislature to place dual purpose tax issues before the voters. In accepting or rejecting the issue, the voter accepts or rejects the package. Boards may present combination issues for (1) current operations and permanent improvements *(O.R.C.6706.217)*, (2) a bond issue with a property tax levy *(O.R.C.5705.218)* and (3) a bond issue with an income tax levy *(O.R.C.5748.08)*.

Conversion Levy for 20-Mill Growth

HB 1 authorizes school districts levying current expense taxes with an aggregate effective tax rate exceeding 20 mills on residential/agricultural real property to convert that excess millage, with voter approval, to a singly levy for a specified amount of money and for a term of up to 10 years or continuously. (The levy conversion would have the effect of suspending future application of the "H.B. 920 tax reduction on the remaining 20 mills for so long as the district does not impose additional current expense millage for other than a fixed amount of money – i.e., new millage other than an "emergency" levy or a renewal of the conversion levy.)

The state is required to reimburse a school district levying a conversion tax for the amount of tax revenue lost from nonresidential/agricultural real property and public utility personal property due to the conversion. The reimbursement is phased out over 13 years in increments equal to 50% of the annual inflationary revenue growth from

The following are actual copies of ballots proposing the passage of an operating levy, bond issue, levy renewal and permanent improvement levy renewal.

31A   PROPOSED TAX LEVY
MAYFIELD CITY SCHOOL DISTRICT
A Majority Affirmative Vote Is Necessary For Passage.

An additional tax for the benefit of the Mayfield City School District for the purpose of CURRENT EXPENSES at a rate not exceeding 0.3 Mill for each one dollar of valuation, which amounts to $0.03 for each one hundred dollars of valuation, for a continuing period of time.

| FOR THE TAX LEVY | 202→ |
| AGAINST THE TAX LEVY | 203→ |

31   PROPOSED BOND ISSUE
MAYFIELD CITY SCHOOL DISTRICT
A Majority Affirmative Vote Is Necessary For Passage.

Shall bonds be issued by the Mayfield City School District for the purpose of

CONSTRUCTING, FURNISHING AND EQUIPPING A SWIMMING POOL, EXPANDED PHYSICAL EDUCATION AND OTHER INSTRUCTIONAL FACILITIES AT MAYFIELD HIGH SCHOOL AND IMPROVING ITS SITE

| FOR THE BOND ISSUE | 196→ |
| AGAINST THE BOND ISSUE | 197→ |

in the sum of Five Million Nine Hundred Thousand ($5,900,000) Dollars and a levy of taxes to be made outside of the ten mill limitation estimated by the County Auditor to average 1.1343 mills for each one dollar of valuation, which amounts to $0.11343 for each one hundred dollars of valuation, for a maximum period of twenty (20) years to pay the principal and interest of such bonds.

24   PROPOSED TAX LEVY—(RENEWAL)
NORTH ROYALTON CITY SCHOOL DISTRICT
A Majority Affirmative Vote Is Necessary For Passage.

A renewal of a tax for the benefit of the North Royalton City School District for the purpose of CURRENT EXPENSES at a rate not exceeding 4.75 Mills for each one dollar of valuation, which amounts to $0.475 for each one hundred dollars of valuation, for two (2) years.

| FOR THE TAX LEVY | 197→ |
| AGAINST THE TAX LEVY | 198→ |

31B   PROPOSED TAX LEVY—(RENEWAL)
MAYFIELD CITY SCHOOL DISTRICT
A Majority Affirmative Vote Is Necessary For Passage.

A renewal of a tax for the benefit of the Mayfield City School District for the purpose of CONSTRUCTING, REMODELING, IMPROVING AND MAKING ADDITIONS TO AND FURNISHING AND EQUIPPING BUILDINGS FOR SCHOOL PURPOSES, INCLUDING VOCATIONAL EDUCATION, AND IMPROVING SCHOOL GROUNDS at a rate not exceeding 0.7 mill for each one dollar of valuation, which amounts to $0.07 for each one hundred dollars of valuation, for five (5) years.

| FOR THE TAX LEVY | 208→ |
| AGAINST THE TAX LEVY | 209→ |

28

residential/agricultural property resulting from the
suspension of the H.B. 920 reduction. Conversions levies and their renewal can be proposed only at a primary or general election.

Further explanation of the conversion levy is given below,
provided by Tom Ash, Legislative Service Director, of the Buckeye
Association of School Administrators:

The Proposed Conversion Levy

	District A	District B
Current Voted Millage	50.80	49.07
Mills that count toward Class I floor	26.05	20.00
Emergency Levies	0	5.90
Total Class I Tax Rate	26.05	25.90

District A would use a conversion levy of 6.05 (26.05 mills – 20
mills) to have continuing growth on the first 20 mills. In essence, the
conversion levy "converts" the 6.05 mills to a fixed sum, or fixed dollar,
levy and allows the 20 mills to grow.

However, there is the issue of differentiated tax reductions factors for Class II and utility tangible personal property values.

The State of Ohio would reimburse District A for the loss of
Class II and utility tangible personal property tax loss for 13 years (basically through 2 reappraisals). The reimbursement would be gradually
phased out during this period. Each time a district passing the conversion levy would experience a reappraisal or update, the amount of
growth in Class I revenues from the update would be determined.

The hold harmless payment would be reduced by one-half of
the amount of the increase in local property taxes on Class I property.
After twelve years of reimbursements, the payments would stop even if
they would not otherwise be fully phased out.

As an added incentive to adopt conversion levies, the tangible
personal property tax reimbursements on any millage that is converted
would be recalculated, and the reimbursement would continue in the
same manner as for emergency levies until the conversion levy would
expire.

Districts must have voter approval of the conversion levy at a
primary or general election before the end of 2014.

Levy for School Safety and Security

HB 59 permits school districts to levy a property tax exclusively for school safety and security purposes. Such levies must comply with all general school levies in excess of the 10 mill limitation. This provision gives local districts an additional option to raise funds at the local level.

School district income taxes

In 1989 the Ohio General Assembly passed Senate Bill 28, a law which gives local boards of education renewed authority to place income taxes for school purposes on the ballot to be voted on by the residents of the school districts. *Ohio Revised Code sections 5748.01 through 5848.06.*

A school district income tax may be approved for any specified number of years or for a continuing period of time. An income tax issue can be placed on the ballot only twice in any one calendar year. A school district income tax with duration of more than five years may be repealed by voter initiative. Repeal efforts can take place only once in any five-year period. Income taxes with duration of five years or less are not subject to voter repeal.

The proceeds of an income tax may be used for any purpose for which property tax proceeds can be used. An income tax may be levied for any amount that district voters are willing to approve, as long as the amount is in increments of .25%. For example an income tax may be levied at .25%, .50%, .75%, 1%, 1.25%, etc.

The income tax for schools is paid by individuals residing in the school district, estates of school district residents and unincorporated businesses located in the district that file Ohio individual income tax returns. Corporations are not subject to the tax.

The basis for the tax is found on line 5 of the Ohio income tax return (Ohio Taxable Income).

Income that is <u>taxed</u> includes: wages, salaries, tips, interest, dividends, unemployment, compensation, self employment, taxable scholarships and fellowships, pensions, annuities, IRA distributions, capital gains, state and local bond interest (except Ohio governments), federal bond interest exempt from federal tax but subject to state tax and alimony received.

Income that is <u>not taxed</u> includes: social security benefits, disability and survivors benefits, railroad retirement benefits, welfare benefits, child support, property received as a gift, bequest or inheritance and workers' compensation.

With the passage of HB 66 in 2005 school districts are now permitted to levy a school district income tax against an alternative tax base that includes only earned income and self-employment income (including income from partnerships): ORC 5748.01(E)(1)(b).

The income tax is not affected by the tax reduction factors in House Bill 920, thus providing an income source which grows with inflation and as the economy expands.

HB 1 (2009) authorizes a school district to combine two or more simultaneously expiring income tax levies into a single renewal levy.

Income taxes had been passed in 172 school districts as of January 2009. Rates range from .5% to 2.0%

Combined city/school income tax

School districts may negotiate an agreement with the local municipality or municipalities, if they have roughly the same boundaries, whereby the municipality places an income tax on the ballot for both municipal and school purposes. At least 25% of the proceeds must be used for school purposes. The issue must be voted on in each municipality involved at the same time and each must pass the issue.

This income tax is paid by individuals who <u>live or work</u> in the municipalities. Further, since it is essentially a payroll tax, pensions, social security, interest, dividends, annuities and income of military personnel are not taxed.

Revenue Sharing - How can this help?

School districts can negotiate revenue sharing agreements with local municipalities that are granting tax abatements for new businesses in the community. In fact, there are some benchmarks established by Ohio Revised Code that require revenue sharing if the new payroll is over $1,000,000. The Board of Education agrees with the abated taxes as long as the municipality "shares" the increase in income taxes, often expressed in a percentage or fixed dollar amount. Some revenue sharing agreements are large enough to hold the school district harmless. In other words, the district collects the same amount it would have collected in real estate tax revenue if the abatement did not exist. Revenue sharing agreements can become a great collaboration between municipalities and school districts.

Local Funding Strategy

Boards of education and their advisors, in considering ways to raise needed funds for schools from local sources, have a complicated mix of factors to consider. The General Assembly has given boards many options. Additionally, certain types of issues are not affected by HB 920, or are given special treatment in law as regards to the 20-mill floor or the 22-mill charge off. The task is to select the kind of tax, the amount of the tax and the timing which will result in a winning vote on election day and still meet the financial needs of the school district.

The board brings an extensive knowledge of the school district and its people to the decision-making process. In making the decision their political knowledge and skills, good judgment and ability to reach a consensus which is publicly supported by all board members must be operating at the highest level. Other than the selection of the superintendent, there is no more important decision which the board makes.

Past Election Results

The Ohio Department of Education, Division of School Finance, keeps excellent records of school election results. You can access these records on their website.

These ODE records will show you what types of issues have the best passing percentages, in the last election and in the past 5 years. The data also show the winning percentages of all issues voted on in May, August and November. These data may help in the selection of the type of funding issue for your district and also in the timing of your issue.

Note: A special thanks to Richard Maxwell for source material in this chapter.

Financing School Construction

The financing of school building construction is generally the responsibility of local boards of education and the citizens whom they represent. Although some state and federal funds are available for specific purposes, such as vocational buildings, only the poorest districts qualify for outside funding. The state has significantly increased its support for school construction through the Ohio Facilities Construction Commission (OFCC) where school districts receive State funding for new construction. The level of State funding is based on ranking list established by the OFCC further described in the following OFCC section.

Local boards may finance building construction either through bonded indebtedness or through pay-as-you-go financing. Let us examine each of these methods.

Bond issues - How do they work?

Bond issues are the most common means used by boards of education to finance new building construction. The major advantage of bond issues is simply that they make the needed funds available immediately. The disadvantage is that the available money is borrowed and interest must be paid on it, usually for long periods of time, often over 30 years.

A successful bond financing relies greatly on three key consultants for the district: a municipal advisor, bond counsel and bond underwriter. A municipal advisor guides the district through the entire process from determining the budget, estimating required millage, interest rate projections, credit ratings, and most importantly representation during the actual sale of the bonds at the financial institution. The attorneys that guide the district with a specialization in school finance related to selling bonds including compliance with the Internal Revenue Service regulations are bond counsel for the district. The bond underwriter is the financial institution selected to perform the sale of the bonds on the cash market underwriting any bonds that are not purchased by investors. All three of these consultants can influence the cost of the bonds through the interest rate ultimately paid by the district. The cost of the municipal advisor, bond counsel and underwriter are paid when the bonds are sold with proceeds from the sale of the bonds. This type of payment is called a transactional payment, the consultants are not paid until the bonds are sold and the transaction is complete.

The process of financing the new buildings through bonds works like this:

• The school board submits a bond issue to the citizens for a vote.
• If the bond issue is approved by the electorate, the board now has a lawful ability to collect the necessary funds to pay for the construction. The board of education will sell bonds in the amount approved by the voters. Since the interest paid on school bonds is tax free, they are generally purchased by wealthy individuals, banks, insurance companies and other big institutions at a relatively low rate of interest. The lawful ability of the board to collect taxes as a result of the bond issue passing is collateral for the bonds.
• The board of education receives all the funds voted on when the bonds are sold and has the money in hand to pay for the new school.
• The board invests the money and draws funds out to pay bills as the construction proceeds. Careful planning and good interest rates can lead to significant interest earnings for the district.
• The board of education uses the yearly proceeds from the bond issue tax levy to make the principal and interest payments based on the schedule established when the bonds were originally sold. This is an amortization schedule that depicts the payments (usually annual or semi-annual) for the finance term (usually 30 to 35 years.)

In many respects the process described above is the way most people purchase a home. They cannot raise the money all at once to pay the total cost of the home. They pay an amount down and borrow the rest of the purchase price from a lending institution. Then they pay back the loan, or mortgage, over a period of years based on a payback schedule (the loan amortization schedule).

Bond issues are generally presented to the people in both dollar amounts and mills. The board of education may be asking for $40 million to build a new high school. The county auditor will figure how many mills will have to be levied to pay back the $40 million bond indebtedness (principal and interest) over a specified period of years, generally 30. With the millage figure local property owners can then compute the initial cost of the bond issue to them if passed.

A very important point about bond issues is that the mills needed to pay them off generally go down each year if property values in the school district increase. As the valuation of property in the school district increases, the number of mills needed to produce the funds necessary to make the payments decreases. For example, if the valuation of property in the district is $500,000,000, two mills will produce

$1,000,000 a year. If in the next year the valuation of property in the district increases to $550,000,000, only 1.8 mills will be needed to produce $1,000,000.

A bond levy is unique since the millage is adjusted each year by the county auditor and school treasurer to ensure that enough tax revenue is raised for the district to pay the annual interest and principal payment. The millage rate can actually increase in a recession of decreasing property values. The millage tax rate is adjusted as the annual payment changes on the amortization schedule (loan payback schedule with the financial institution). Districts often refinance bonds in order to lock in better interest rates, just as individuals refinance their home mortgages. Usually the refinance terms are in the original bond finance structure or the municipal advisor will recommend certain times in the payback period where the district will have the opportunity to refinance. The majority of bond issues for school districts are tax exempt providing tax advantages for the investor and competitive interest rates for the district. Bond counsel will ensure that the district complies with the Federal IRS regulations associated with tax exempt bonds.

Investing Bond Issue Funds

When school districts sell bonds for a building program, they receive the entire amount of the bond issue when the bonds are sold. This money will immediately be invested, perhaps at a higher interest rate that the tax free bonds were sold for. Federal IRS regulations have established limits on interest revenue earned while bond proceeds are invested in order to maintain the tax exempt status. Bond counsel will ensure the district is in compliance with the Federal IRS regulations. The district must also spend bond proceeds during construction period within certain timelines required by the IRS in order to preserve the tax exempt status.

Building programs usually take several years. Traditionally the longer money is invested, the higher the interest rate. The treasurer will calculate when the bond issue money will be needed to pay for the construction as it progresses and invest accordingly. Some of the money may be invested for a month or more. Some for several years.

Another fact about bond issues is that interest which will be earned is usually not considered to be part of income when the bond issue is structured. There is no way to know what the exact interest rate will be so the amount earned cannot be accurately predicted. However, interest will be earned. This income may be used for unexpected contingencies. More commonly, it will be used for something the public might be reluctant to vote for. Since whatever it is used for can be publicized as "free," out of interest earnings and not paid for by taxpayers, usually the decision on how to spend the money is well accepted.

Pay-as-you-go - How does it work?

If a family has a 20-year mortgage on its home, it will probably end up paying more than double the true cost of the home because of the interest it must pay on borrowed money. The family might be better off, assuming a low rate of inflation, if they pay the entire cost of the home at purchase time and not borrow money. Schools are in the same position.

Some school districts, generally those in very wealthy areas or those in areas which are not growing substantially, can meet their needs on a pay-as-you-go basis. They pay for their new facilities as they build them. They pay no interest costs. Over a long period of time their schools will only cost about half as much to build as those in districts which use bonded indebtedness.

Pay-as-you-go issues are often called permanent improvement levies. They will be presented in terms of dollars (will raise $100,000 per year) or in terms of mills (two mills per year). The millage rate allows taxpayers to compute how much the levy will cost them. Such levies may be voted on for a period of one to five years or, if the levies are for on-going improvements, for a continuing period of time. The school district will accumulate enough funds for the building project through the permanent improvement fund after years of saving for the entire building or construct improvement additions to existing buildings as the district can afford with the yearly revenue.

Buildings without ballots

In 1998 the Legislature passed a law (R.C. 5705-314) which allows districts, meeting certain requirements, to build buildings without the need to pass a bond issue. The law permits a board of education to move all or part of its inside millage out of the general fund revenue category to the permanent improvement fund.

A prior law prohibits the auditor from reducing a districts' general fund millage below 20 effective mills. These 20 mills are a combination of inside (unvoted) and outside (voted) millage. It would be normal for districts to have about 4.5 inside mills in the general operating fund category.

In a procedure clearly requiring legal help, the board, after a public hearing, may transfer all or part of its inside millage from the general operating fund to the Permanent Improvement fund. This will bring the operating fund below 20 effective mills. The auditor, without a vote of the people, will then increase taxes in the amount of the inside millage which has been transferred out, bringing the operating fund back up to the required 20 mills.

The board may then form a non-profit corporation which borrows money from a bank using the recently transferred inside millage as collateral. The corporation builds the school and leases it to the board. Proceeds from the transferred millage are used to make the lease payments. At the end of the lease period, after the lease is paid off, the board owns the school.

Boards should be aware that, on December 2 of 2014 in *Sanborn V. Hamilton County Budget Commission,* the Ohio Supreme Court made it clear that the budget commission must find that reallocation of this millage is "clearly required," which is the standard for approval of all levies.

Certificates of Participation

Another option for school districts to finance new buildings without a taxpayer ballot is a Certificates of Participation (COPs) deal. A COPs financing requires substantial documentation, municipal fund advisor services, and bond counsel expertise. Public certificates of participation are sold where investors own the new school building while the district is the lessee promising to appropriate the lease payment for the future agreed upon finance term. A COPs deal is a great alternative for school districts seeking new buildings. This type of financing is accepted by the Ohio Facilities Construction Commission. All in all, the district has to present the financial capacity or revenue streams that will pay for the lease payments into the future. The good news is that the district gets new buildings with no taxpayer vote as required by a bond levy.

Tax Anticipation Notes

Because property taxes levied by school districts provide a relatively secure source of revenue over the life of the tax issue, Ohio Revised Code 133.24 (Tax Anticipation Notes) allows boards of education to borrow against the future proceeds of certain types of tax issues, such as inside millage or permanent improvement levies. The advantage of this financial tactic is to allow boards to sell tax anticipation notes, giving them the funds to undertake major construction or renovation projects in the first year that the tax is being collected, same as would be true of a bond issue. In following years, the boards use the proceeds of the tax issue to pay off the tax anticipation notes. Another advantage, such as in the case of Permanent Improvement levies of limited duration, is that at the expiration of the levy, the board can present the P.I. levy to the voters as a renewal, rather than a new bond issue or tax increase, then issue tax anticipation notes following passage of the levy.

Ohio Facilities Construction Commission (OFCC)

In order to better deal with the problem of inadequate school facilities, in May of 1997 the Legislature passed Senate Bill 102 (122nd General Assembly) which created the *Ohio School Facilities Commission (OSFC)*. The Commission is the action arm of the Legislature in efficiently turning significant additional funding into school facility improvements.

In 2012 the Ohio School Facilities Commission and the Office of the State Architect were merged, creating a new organization, *the Ohio Facilities Construction Commission* (OFCC). The merger combined the state's construction authority and resources into a single entity that guides capital projects for many state agencies, including most of Ohio's public kindergarten through twelfth grade (K-12) schools.

The mission of the new organization is "To lead collaboration with our partners in the planning, design, and construction of public facilities through quality service, expertise, and knowledge sharing."

The new Commission sets uniform rules, procedures, and standardized documents for public construction, and is responsible for construction delivery methods, construction documents and process and procedures.

The areas where the commission assists local school districts are:

*The Classroom Facilities Assistance Program (CFAP). This is by far the biggest program and has helped school districts all over Ohio.

*Expedited Local Partnership Program (ELPP). This program allows districts not yet able to qualify for CFAP to move ahead with a needed building program and receive credit for all expenditure when they do move on to the approved list.

*Exceptional Needs Program (ENP). Allows eligible applicants to replace buildings most in need of replacement.

*Vocational Facilities Assistance Program (VFAP). Similar to the CFAP, but for Joint Vocational School Districts.

*Vocational Facilities Assistance Expedited Local Partnership (VFAP-ELPP). Similar to the ELPP, but for Vocational School Districts.

The largest area of service is in Classroom Facilities Assistance. Schools are granted state funds primarily according to their placement on an equity list provided by the ODE. It is based on local property wealth per pupil. The poorest districts receive the highest priority and also receive a higher percentage of state aid for their construction projects. After placement on the approved list, districts have a year to pass a local issue to help pay the local share of construction. The local issue also assures funds will be available to maintain the new facilities.

The impact of the OFCC upon Ohio school facilities has been nothing short of remarkable. When the DeRolph case was filed in 1991

38

a national commission rated Ohio school facilities to be the worst in the nation. Since then over $12 billion has been allocated to the program by the Legislature and spent. Since its inception, the OFCC has worked with more than seventy five percent of the state's public school districts.

On July 8 of 2021 the OFCC approved $242 million in state funds for nine public school construction projects, combined with $208 million in local funds for a total of $450 million for school facilities improvements.

Since its inception, the Commission has helped pay for over a thousand schools buildings in about half the school districts in the state. It would be difficult to drive very far in any direction in Ohio and not see a school building either built or renovated with the help of OFCC state money.

It is the stated aim of the OFCC to build buildings, using quality construction, for 21st century education.

The Commission approaches its role as "Local control with state oversight." The Commission has brought a high level of professionalism to Ohio school construction. They assess building needs. They have developed a school design manual, which establishes standards regarding classroom and other spaces, as well as the functions which can be performed in those spaces. For example, cafeterias are allowed to be built with state money, but not auditoriums. Thus we have the hybrid space of "cafetoriums," which serve as both cafeterias and auditoriums.

The OFCC employs a construction manager for all classroom projects. Each project is also placed on the internet. Any citizen with a computer can observe the progress of any project. A secure section of the website allows contractors, owners, the state and other principals to trade information.

State Support of Education

The founding fathers of our nation made no specific mention of education in the United States Constitution. The 10th amendment says, "The powers not delegated to the United States by the Constitution, nor prohibited by it to the States, are reserved to the States respectively, or to the people." Education became a state function. Thus, we have 50 systems for providing for public education in the country, one for each state.

The Constitution of the State of Ohio requires that the General Assembly "shall make such provisions, by taxation or otherwise, that will secure a thorough and efficient system of common schools throughout the state." The words "thorough and efficient," as they relate to schools, are found in many state constitutions. They are the basis for most of the school finance lawsuits which have swept the country in the last several decades, including the DeRolph case here in Ohio. The Legislature makes laws regarding all aspects of schooling; educational and operational, as well as financial.

History of state funding in Ohio

Prior to the 1930's, financial support for Ohio schools came primarily from the real property tax and revenue from school lands. In 1935, as Ohio adopted its first state school foundation program, the General Assembly assumed responsibility for providing a basic level of state support for education. In that year, a 3% sales tax was enacted and its proceeds, applied to education, increased state support from almost nothing to 50% of the operating costs. By 1970, however, the school operating costs financed by the state had dropped to about 33%.

In 1971, the Ohio General Assembly passed the first state income tax. The tax has since provided many billions of dollars for elementary and secondary education, both public and private, and for other state activities and services. (As indicated in a 1981 enactment, it is the intent of the General Assembly that the personal income tax money is to be used for primary and secondary education.)

In 1975, the Ohio General Assembly passed a new "equal yield formula" designed to increase state funding for schools while at the same time compensating for differences in local taxable wealth. Under the equal yield approach each school district would receive the same amount of money per pupil (local and state combined) for each mill levied up to 30 mills. By 1980, with the per pupil amount of state funding increasing each year, approximately 45% of the total operating cost of public education was borne by the state.

In 1998 the Legislature passed HB650, the new foundation program. It was intended to be a "cost-based" model of state funding for schools. That is, the money provided by the state was intended to be based on what it actually costs to provide an adequate education for each public school student in Ohio. The prior model, according to testimony in the DeRolph case, was really a "budgetary residual" model. The state met its other financial obligations first and then allocated the money remaining to schools, using a foundation formula which was adjusted to produce a financial obligation which the Legislature was willing to fund. In the "cost based" model the state financial obligation is first established, then the money necessary to fund that model is provided by the Legislature, even if tax increases or cuts in other state-assisted programs are required. As the reader can see, the difference between the two approaches is significant.

State funding continued from that point as a funding formula calculating the funding amount for each public school district in Ohio. The funding formula utilized various factors and indexes based on student enrollment, poverty levels, property values and the income level of taxpayers within the respective district. One would conclude that changes in enrollment or the other factors listed above would increase or decrease the level of State funding. However, as the formula progressed in history, a cap on the growth in funding and a guarantee on the decrease in funding were added to protect districts from wide swings in State funding. Over time the cap in funding (maximum growth rate) would under fund districts with substantial growth in enrollment and the guarantee would over fund districts that were reduced in size due the decreases in enrollment. Fast forward to FY2021, more than two thirds of the districts were on the cap or guarantee; truly depicting a malfunctioning funding formula. Adding the multiple biennium budgets with frozen State funding or the recent reduced State funding in FY2020 due to the COVID 19 Pandemic, the State funding formula was overdue for a rehaul. The Fair School Funding Formula was established by a broad coalition of school people to propose a fix for the State funding formula in 2019 with an eye on future biennium budgets in Ohio. The Fair School Funding Formula was incorporated into the 2022-2023 biennium budget and is described in the section on 134th General Assembly.

Factors in the State Funding Process

It is likely that all states have to deal with common factors in school funding and go through a similar process. The steps are:

• Determine, in some fashion, how much it will cost to provide a minimum, basic education for every child in the state.

    • Add funds for programs that cost more than the basic amount, such as vocational or special education, targeted assistance, or other items the legislature wishes to support, such as transportation or alternatives to public schools.

    • Determine the amount that the state will pay of the above.

    • Multiply the state percentage amount by ADM or other relevant factors, such as miles traveled by busses.

    • Apply guarantees so school income will not be reduced and caps so increases will be modest.

Budgeting for Schools is an Educational- Financial-Political Process

One should appreciate the democratic complexity of the school funding process as it advances from the proposal first put forth by the Governor's office. It is then sent to the House of Representatives for study and amendment, then to the Senate for similar study and amendment, then to a joint committee and then, for final approval, to the Governor, who has line item veto power. Governor Kasich vetoed 47 line items from HB49. The final two year (biennium) budget plan, of which education funding will be the third largest segment of the state budget, must be adopted by June 30th.

All segments of education are well represented in the process. The Ohio School Boards Association, the Buckeye Association of School Administrators, The Ohio Association of Public School Employees, the Ohio Education Association, The American Federation of Teachers, the Parent Teacher Associations, and others, have highly skilled and knowledgably representatives working to shape a budget which they consider to be fair and workable.

During the lengthy review and revision process, as new proposals are made, computer printouts are run and disseminated which show how each new plan will financially affect every school district in the state. District leaders review the printouts and make their views known to their representatives. The state legislators, who must approve the final budget, also watch these printouts closely, each looking out for the interests of the school districts they represent. In the end, a school finance plan is adopted, the best one the legislative process can create.

Targeted funding

The primary reason the Ohio school finance system is so complex is that the legislature attempts to craft the system to accomplish specific goals, solve specific problems or help specific constituencies.

The Legislature could simply take the available state money, divide it by the number of public school pupils, give each school district a flat sum of money based on their enrollment and allow the local districts to spend the state money as they think best.

In fact, for decades the state foundation formula worked out in that way. Enrollment was multiplied by an amount which the state determined and that provided the bulk of state funding to the local districts.

Then refinements were added. Today it would be impossible for the Ohio Department of Education to implement the school funding law without the aid of powerful computers.

Thorough and efficient/adequate and equitable

The state constitution mandates that the legislature provide our state with a public school system which is *thorough and efficient*. These terms were the basis of the DeRolph litigation. They are difficult to define precisely. Over time, they have come to be replaced by two other terms, also difficult to define, but which have become generally accepted as quality standards for school finance systems. They are:

Adequate-Are we spending *enough* or *the proper amount* on our schools, and
Equitable- Are we allocating the available funds *fairly*.

Adequacy

Previous legislatures and governors have taken on the difficult task of determining an adequate level of funding for our schools using different approaches, always with the practical requirement that the state must have the necessary funds to pay for the adequacy level which the underlying method produces. It could be viewed that an adequate level of funding for education is the same amount as our taxpayers are willing to pay to support our schools.

Equity

Regarding the equity standard, the Legislature must deal with the 500 pound gorilla of Ohio school funding - local property tax wealth. Local income in school districts can be reduced to a simple formula of (taxable property value x school tax rate = local school income). There is a wide difference in property tax wealth among Ohio school districts, and in local school tax rates. The Ohio finance system relies heavily on the property tax to fund schools. These local differences simply overpower the state equalization effort.

The current equity concept of the Legislature is that the funding of schools should be a partnership between the State and local school districts. The concept of "local control" is one we hear often. Accordingly, the Ohio funding plan includes several measures to assure that the local districts pay their share.

• Every district must levy at least 20 authorized mills for current operations locally in order to receive any state funds. This is called the 20-mill qualifier. Every district in Ohio does levy at least 20 mills for current operations.

• After the basic funding amount is determined the state takes into account an "average valuation" factor and a "district income" factor and determines a "state-share index," which is the percentage the state will pay. This makes the funding a combination of state and local money. The greater the share of the formula amount which can be raised locally, the less the state will give the district in basic aid (called the Opportunity Grant) and vice versa. The formula is intended to help equalize educational funding around the state.

The graph to the right shows the concept.

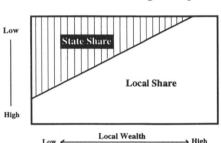

Ohio School Funding Concept

How does the State pay for Public Schools?

The State pays for primary and secondary education with various funds (revenue sources), with the GRF (General Revenue Fund) covering 72% of the total cost. The Ohio Lottery, Tangible Personal Property Tax reimbursements, Property Tax Reimbursements, and Student Wellness and Success funds cover the remaining cost. Property Tax Reimbursements are for the rollback discounts tax payers receive for personal residence, discussed in the Important Concepts of Local School Finance chapter of this book.

BASIC ELEMENTS OF AMENDED SUBSTITUTE

State Funding to Ohio Public Schools

The State pays for the cost of Primary and Secondary Education Funding with the following funds:

State GRF
Ohio Lottery
TPP Reimbursement
Property Tax Reimbursement
Student Wellness and Success

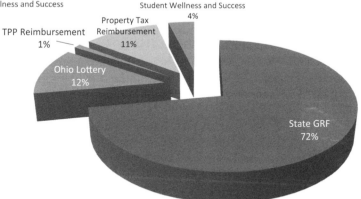

State Funding to Ohio Public Schools: How the State Pays

Student Wellness and Success 4%
Property Tax Reimbursement 11%
TPP Reimbursement 1%
Ohio Lottery 12%
State GRF 72%

HOUSE BILL 110, THE OHIO SCHOOL FINANCE BILL AS PASSED BY THE 134TH GENERAL ASSEMBLY AND SIGNED BY GOVERNOR MIKE DEWINE.

Fair School Funding Plan

Educators in Ohio have long wanted a state foundation formula based on what it actually costs to educate a student in the public schools of this state.

The Fair School Funding Plan was created almost two years ago by a large work group of Ohio school finance leaders (treasurers, super-intendents and other administration) and State Representatives Cupp and Patterson.

The workgroup was organized, and made recommendations, based on major State funding issues such as: base cost of education, special education, transportation, open enrollment, economic disad-vantaged funds and student wellness. The Fair School Funding Plan is included in HB110; establishing a funding formula based on the cost of educating students in each respective school district.

Direct funding of community schools, STEM Schools and State scholarship programs

Prior public school funding formulas counted the entire student population within the school district no matter where the student attended school; such as non-public schools, community schools, Ed Choice or other scholarship programs; then DEDUCTED the money going to non-public school students from the public school funding amount. This made it appear that non -public schools were receiving money that public schools were actually entitled to.

The Fair School Funding Plan eliminates this process, by funding public schools based on the actual students that the school district educates. Community schools, STEM schools, and State scholarships awarded under the Ed Choice, Autism, and Jon Peterson Special Needs program will be paid for directly from the State without passing through public school district funding formulas.

Implementation of the new formula phase- in for State funding

The Fair School Funding Plan has a six-year phase in period, thus FY 2022 and FY 2023 will see the first two years of the phase in. This is due to the ultimate increase in the cost of the formula to the State. The Governor vetoed the automatic continuance of the plan into the future by establishing language that the General Assembly will determine the calculations of the formula for FY 2024 and thereafter.

The general phase-in percentages for the formula amount for FY 2022 and FY 2023 are 16.67% and 33.33% respectively. The statewide total cost after the phase-in percentages results in $7.08B for FY 2022 and $7.15B for FY 2023.

In comparison, the total cost of the new formula at 100% is $10.9B for the first fiscal year with the average base cost per pupil at $7,202. The FY 2021 base cost per student was $6,020, substantially less than the new formula at 100%. The school foundation formula, in recent memory, has not been funded at 100%.

It is important that the State prioritizes the funding of public education in order to reach the goal of a 100% phase -in of the funding formula within six years as this funding plan calls for.

Base Cost for Traditional School Districts

HB110 establishes a base cost that replaces the prior formula amount ($6,020 per pupil) with a variable base cost computed for each school district. The base cost is made up of various components including: teacher salaries, student support, district leadership, accountability, building operations and athletic co-curricular activities. The calculation takes these district components and combines that data with statewide average staff and teacher salaries, student to teacher ratios, district spending data and district insurance costs.

Average salaries and costs within the calculation are based on FY 2018 data. HB110 modifies how students are counted for State funding specifying that the base cost enrolled is equal to the district's enrolled ADM from the prior fiscal year or the average of the district's enrolled ADM for the prior three fiscal years. The prior formula ADM included all students residing in the district, including community school, STEM, Ed Choice, Jon Peterson, Autism scholarship and any public school not part of the district. The total cost of the new formula is $10.9B for the first fiscal year with the average base cost per pupil at $7,202; this is prior to the six-year phase in as discussed above.

State Share Index

The State Share Index is used to equalize State funding payments based upon the district's capacity to raise local revenue (tax revenue). As the index is applied to the funding formula, lower wealth districts receive more funds and higher wealth districts receive less. HB110 establishes a calculation for the State share index by utilizing three key factors: valuation per pupil, federally adjusted gross income (FAGI) per pupil local capacity and the adjusted FAGI per pupil.

The index ranks all districts based on the median federally adjusted gross income (FAGI) for the most recent year available and property valuation per pupil. The Statewide averages per pupil local capacity amount is estimated at $4,121 in FY 2022 and $4,457 in FY 2023. This is the primary way the formula attempts to equalize funding in each Ohio school district.

Transportation

It would surprise most people to know that the state law requires districts to transport only those students in grades K-8 who live more than two miles from the school they attend. Yet virtually all districts have expensive transportation facilities, transporting their own students K-12, JVS students, non-public students and community school students.

HB110 recognized the additional cost of transporting students not enrolled at the district by providing a 1.5 per student weighted funding for community school and STEM school students transported and 2.0 per student weighted funding for non-public students. HB110 also bases the funding on 28 riders per mile density.

Formula transition supplement and temporary transitional aid

In past biennium budgets the State funding for individual districts would be adjusted for a guarantee of no decrease in funding or a cap on the growth in funding. Over the years these adjustments resulted in over two thirds of the school districts on a guarantee or cap (not on the funding formula created for public school districts). The formula was not working as it was designed to operate. HB110 will provide a formula transition supplement for districts as the new formula is phased in. The formula transition supplement will cost $112.5M in FY 2022 and $81.2M in FY 2023. HB110 guarantees that districts will not see any decrease in their funding base for FY 2021. The funding base for FY 2021 includes the following:

1. FY 2021 foundation aid before any State budget reductions ordered by the Governor
2. Less transfers for students attending community or STEM schools
3. Less the cost of scholarships for students in the Ed Choice, Autism, and Jon Peterson Special Needs programs
4. Adjustment for students open enrolling
5. Add the FY 2021 student wellness and success funds and enhancement funds
6. Add the enrollment growth supplement for FY 2021

Another temporary transitional aid guarantee and cap is established for the phase in for districts that have a decrease in incoming open enrollment students. If a district has the greater of a decrease in 20 incoming open enrollment students or a 10% decrease in open enrollment students, the guaranteed funding will be reduced. The statewide total for temporary transitional aid is $71.6m for FY 2022 and $177.8M for FY 2023.

Career Awareness and Exploration Funds

HB110 earmarks $4.2M in FY 2022 and $8.4M in FY 2023 for career awareness and exploration funds to be distributed outside of the school funding formula to traditional districts, JVSD's, community and STEM schools. The funding is based on an amount equal to the school enrollment times $2.50 for FY 2022, $5 for FY 2023, $7.50 for FY 2024, and $10 for FY 2025 and each fiscal year thereafter. The funds are for specific purpose with plans established by the Career Technical Planning District of which the school district belongs.

Other components of HB110 State funding of public schools

HB110 changes the six categories of special education funding and the weighted multiples. The district's state share percentage is used for the special education funding instead of the state share index as in the prior years.

The statewide total for special education additional aid is $766M in FY 2022 and $746.4M in FY 2023. The disadvantaged pupil impact aid is increased from $272 to $422 per pupil base with a total cost of $620.5M in each fiscal year. Gifted funds will receive $83.7M in FY 2022 and $79.2M in FY 2023 via the new formula. The statewide total for career-technical funding is $54.3M in FY 2022 and $53.7M in FY 2023 through the formula.

Student success and wellness funding will continue within the formula and the executive appropriation will be redirected to paying for disadvantaged pupil impact aid. Early childhood programs will receive $68.1M in both FY 2022 and FY 2023. The total funding for JVSDs is $344.1M in FY 2022 and $365.2M in FY 2023.

HB110 is initiating great changes in the State funding of public education in Ohio. The overhaul of the prior funding formula was long desired by educators. This may be the first time in Ohio School Finance where the school districts provided the research, data and formula solution to the State. The State's recognition of this hard work by the FSFP is evidenced by the Legislature passing, and the Governor adopting, the new funding formula in HB110.

As the partnership continues, the aim is to properly fund schools in order to provide effective elementary and secondary school education for all Ohio students.

Main Operating Budget					
House Bill 110 Budget (dollars in millions)					
Program Category	FY 2021	FY 2022	% change	FY 2023	% change
K-12 Education	$9,437.0	$9,803.9	3.7%	$9,749.0	-0.6%
Medicaid	$16,518.0	$16,441.3	-0.5%	$20,340.8	19.2%
Health & Human Services	$1,367.0	$1,629.3	16.1%	$1,610.9	-1.1%
Higher Education	$2,583.9	$2,738.7	5.7%	$2,743.5	0.2%
Corrections (Dept. Rehab & Youth Services)	$2,098.7	$2,179.2	3.7%	$2,258.0	3.5%
General Government	$2,182.7	$2,381.2	8.3%	$2,387.8	0.3%
GRF Program Total	$9,437.0	$35,173.6	2.8%	$39,090.0	10.0%

Reductions in State Aid

Once a district's state aid is established, the amount is not guaranteed for a year. The Governor, by executive order, may reduce the state aid level. This has occurred several times, the most recent being in 2020 when Governor DeWine cut 300 million from the elementary and secondary budget due to the economics of the COVID19 Pandemic. The reductions were applied to the last four payments of foundation aid for May and June of 2020. Some districts actually owed funds back to the State, while other districts absorbed the loss of State funds. Further reductions were slated for FY 2021, but eventually cancelled as the economic impact of the COVID19 Pandemic was not as bad as originally anticipated.

THE IMAGE PROBLEM FOR THE GOVERNOR AND LEGISLATURE

There is a general conception in Ohio, thanks mostly to the DeRolph litigation, that the Ohio school funding system is broken. Each governor and legislature attempts to fix it, or have it appear that they have fixed it. In reality, the system consists of a series of choices which our political leaders have made. Other choices, other approaches, could be made but the factors our legislators are dealing with do not change. The choices are primarily driven by a desire to improve our schools, by political considerations and are limited by budgetary constraints.

In the end, no matter the series of different approaches and different names given to the approaches the funds given to the local schools have not changed much from year to year. With the formula calculations, guarantees and caps the bottom line funding number always equals what the legislature has to spend, or is willing to spend, on our public schools. Traditionally that amount is limited to the amount of increased state tax receipts. Legislators are not willing to shift money from other state functions or increase state taxes.

The Ohio system relies heavily on the local property tax, as do many other states. Probably this is true because legislators would rather have local school boards tax our residents for education than do it themselves. Raising taxes places legislative jobs in jeopardy.

For many years our legislature has created school finance formulas and did not fund them fully, sometimes openly and sometimes by tinkering with elements of the funding formula. To educators in the field, this smacks of cheating.

Recent funding bills take a great deal of money from public schools and sends it to alternative educational choices such as community schools, private schools and electronic schools. The amount was 909 million in HB64. This has been a trend in Ohio in the recent past. This is an affront to public school educators. They question the political motives.

The FY 2016-2107 school foundation program (HB 64) may have been a turning point. There is never enough money available to make everyone happy. But HB64 was both technically sophisticated and progressive. Perhaps the advancing power of technology has finally allowed the legislature to factor enough elements into the formula that leaders of fewer districts feel that their circumstances and needs have not been addressed.

The big differences in local property wealth available to support schools in Ohio districts are not going way. The legislature continues to work items into the formula to further foster equity.

The improving economy has meant an increase in state tax receipts. This allows the legislature to provide more money for the poorer districts in the state while holding the wealthier districts harmless under guarantees, without raising taxes and without diminishing the funding for the multitude of other functions which the state supports financially.

The Ohio Legislative Service Commission is the hard working agency that assists the legislature in the budget process. Much of the information in this state aid section of the book comes from them. They publish a detailed explanation of the school funding program called "School Funding Complete Resource." This publication not only includes complete explanations of how the program works, but also includes the actual formulas used in the foundation calculations as well as many charts and graphs. They also provide public simulations of the proposed foundation program so leaders in each district know how the formula being considered at the time will impact their district.

This agency also provides an excellent analysis of all bills as the bills move through the legislative process. They win high praise from all quarters for their expertise and excellent level of service.

The legislators count on feedback from the people being affected by the foundation program. Subcommittees hold hearings and allow organizations which represent educators, parents, taxpayers of anyone else, to have their say.

There is an old saying in politics that "You are either at the table or on the menu." Educators have clout at the table through our professional organizations. Legislators need that input in order to make good laws and good laws benefit us all.

Federal Aid to Education

When the U.S. Constitution was written, education was not mentioned. Thus education became a state function. Although there are many commonalities, each of our states has developed their own education system, with objectives, funding and administration specific to each state.

However, education has always been a national concern. Throughout our history the federal government has taken measures to assist schools and promote education of the populace.

In the early days of the nation the federal government owned the land in the western territories. Part of this land was set aside for support of public education. In these days the new territories were organized into townships, 6 miles by 6 miles.

Township

6 miles ⟶

6	5	4	3	2	1
7	8	9	10	11	12
18	17	**16**	15	14	13
19	20	21	22	23	24
30	29	28	27	26	25
31	32	33	34	35	36

Each township had 36 sections. Each section was one mile square, 640 acres of land. The Northwest Ordinance of 1785 contained the famous "Section 16" Provision. States were directed to set aside the 16th section of each township for the support of public schools.

The Northwest Ordinance of 1787 contained language which clearly shows the federal mandate in support of public education. Often attributed to Thomas Jefferson, it states, in part:

"Religion, morality and knowledge being necessary to a good government and the happiness of mankind, schools and the means of education shall forever be encouraged."

The phrase "schools and the means of education shall forever be encouraged" should be remembered by those who support our public schools and held up to the leaders of today as an example of enlightened thinking.

Many federal programs have been created as a result of external social forces rather than from the primary needs of education. World War I influenced the Smith-Hughes Vocational Education Act; massive demobilization after World War II led to the GI Bill, and the launch of the Russian satellite Sputnik sparked the National Defense Education Act of 1958.

Basic Elements of Federal Aid

Although there may be exceptions, the following general aspects of federal funding continue to apply, some in response to state and federal requirements:

- The majority of federal funds available to schools flows through the Office of Federal Programs which is an extension of the Ohio Department of Education. They have an extensive web based system of federal fund eligibility, compliance, accounting, and enforcement. All other federal funds are normally accessed as sub grants from other federal, state, or local agencies such as Ohio Jobs and Family Services, Ohio Environmental Protection Agency, county or municipal governments, etc.
- Schools must develop a plan for the use of its federal funds in consultation with teachers, administrators, parents, and other community members. These plans must include goals and measures, be made available to the public, and in some instances require a public hearing. Further the plan must include non-public or alternate schools if they educate eligible students that reside in the public school district boundaries. An evaluation of the plan and whether the goals have been met is normally determined by test data results and/or compliance audits performed by the administering agency.
- Due to the prescriptive nature of the federal and state guidelines for use of federal funds at the local level, discretion is often limited.
- Federal funds are committed for limited durations and are typically limited to one-year, which usually coincides with a school district's fiscal year of July 1 to June 30. Many federal programs include carryover provisions for an additional one year period. However, some are uniquely limited to one 12-month period. The theory is that the funds

should be used to support the needs of the current students.

- Federal funds cannot be used to supplant (take the place of) existing programs and must supplement (add to) new or existing programs. Calculations by local officials are prepared annually to ensure that these relationships are maintained. One needs to be careful during non-federal budget reductions that the supplant barrier is not crossed. The penalty for supplanting local with federal funds is a 10% reduction to the federal allocation.
- Federal funds are administered on an expenditure reimbursement basis, meaning that the school incurs the expense and then submits documents to the awarding agency to then be reimbursed. Further, these expenses must be incurred (transacted) within the grant period and no pre or post payments are permitted.
- Schools must maintain control and title to any and all materials, equipment, and property purchased and ensure that federal funds are not used for religious purposes.
- Compliance monitoring is added emphasis under the Elementary and Secondary Education Act (ESEA) programs and is conducted by the Ohio Department of Education's Office of Federal Programs using a tiered review approach involving school self-survey, consultant desk top review, and consultant on-site inspection. Non-compliance findings result in the school submission in writing of a corrective action plan with review, resolution, and acceptance by ODE.

One of the largest federal aid programs for a school district is Title I Part A funding, which is restricted to providing funds to improve the educational programs for districts with high levels of poverty.

Another Federal Aid Grant is Title IIA, which is for improving the quality of teachers and principals to ultimately impact the success of students in the classroom. School districts receive funds for teachers and principals to attend professional development. The grant can also be utilized to recruit and retain highly qualified teachers and principals for the school district.

Federal Grants in Aid can provide vital funding for school districts that do not have the financial capacity to raise local tax revenue. Federal Grants in Aid provide funds for many programs such as Title III Limited English Proficiency, Title I School Improvement, Title VIB Rural and Low Income, and the Federal Breakfast and Lunch Program.

There are also various State grants for restricted programs such as: Preschool Early Childhood Education, Improving Education through Technology, and Career Technical Adult Education. The State funds follow the same process as noted above for Federal Aid Funds through the CCIP program at the ODE.

History of Federal Aid

THE ELEMENTARY AND SECONDARY EDUCATION ACT OF 1965 (ESEA) is the granddaddy of modern federal legislation regarding public schools. It was part of President Lyndon B. Johnson's "Great Society" program. Johnson had the ambitious aim of eliminating poverty in America. A good place to start was in the public schools. ESEA directed funds towards children from lower income families and provided other services toward providing equality of educational opportunity.

With every reauthorization since 1965 congress built on and revised ESEA. They listened to local and state officials. They attempted to improve the effectiveness of the federal spending and serve the priorities of the party in power. As with all legislation, a law once passed remains in effect until it is revised or overturned by a newer law. Many elements of ESEA, and all succeeding laws, remain in effect today.

The EDUCATION CONSOLIDATION AND IMPROVEMENT ACT OF 1981 updated ESEA. Under President Ronald Reagan, the primary aim of this legislation was to reduce federal regulation and shift authority and responsibility on to state and local officials.

NO CHILD LEFT BEHIND ACT OF 2001. (NCLBA)Passed under President George Bush, ushered in a new and unprecedented level of federal involvement and control. NCLB (P.L. 107-110, H.R.1) is nearly 1,000 pages long and has 10 titles or major sections. Its 4 major themes focused on provisions designed to increase accountability by requiring more testing of student achievement; giving parents and students more choices by allowing them to opt out of failing schools; gave states, school districts and schools greater flexibility in how federal funds were to be allocated and put reading first by providing special help to student who were not reading at grade level by the third grade.

RACE TO THE TOP PROGRAM OF 2009. This Obama era program provided grant money to states that agreed to adopt national curriculum standards and other quality measures.

ENSURING STUDENT SUCCESS ACT OF 2016. (ESSA)Passed under President Barack Obama but with a Republican congress, this act provides a major change in the focus of federal aid to schools.

The election of Donald Trump as President in 2017 and his selection of Betsy DeVos as Secretary of Education gave the President, through his budget recommendations, the ability to influence funding of ESSA to support current administrative goals for elementary and secondary education.

A first priority is a reduction in the size and budget of the Department of Education. In fiscal 1989 the Department was allocated $17.1 billion. This grew to $68.3 billion in FY 2016. The President requests $59 billion in FY 2018, a reduction of 13% below the FY 2017 level.

The FY 2018 budget proposed elimination of 22 federally funded programs.

The other major priority involves an expansion of school choice, combined with budget priorities to facilitate this.

In his Fiscal Year 2018 budget message, the President writes, "I am calling upon members of both parties to pass an education bill that funds school choice for disadvantaged youth…These families should be free to choose the public, private, charter, magnet, religious or home school that is right for them."

In the budget summary we read, "The 2018 President's Budget would provide robust funding for the President's top priority of ensuring that every child has the opportunity to attend a high quality school selected by his or her parents…"

The primary funding method for implementing school choice is for the money to follow the student, whose parents will decide how it should be spent, rather than giving the money to the school, or other educational organization, for distribution. This is called portable public education funding.

Secretary of Education Betsy DeVos, speaking at the Brookings Institute in March of 2017 said, "..we must shift the paradigm to think about education funding as investments made in individual children, not in institutions or buildings."

Other federal education programs in Ohio

- School Food Service program - Nearly every Ohio child who purchases a meal or a container of milk in a school cafeteria has a part of the cost of the food subsidized by one of several federal programs. These programs either provide free food to use in regular school lunches, or reimburse the school for part of the cost of milk and food sold in school cafeterias. In addition to the subsidies, thousands of needy Ohio school children receive free breakfasts and/or lunches in school cafeterias, part or all of the cost of which is paid for from federal sources or all of the cost of which is paid from federal sources. In 2016 the Department of Agriculture spent $22 billion on school lunches and related programs.
- Vocational Education - Federal funding is provided for a broad range

of vocationally related projects, ranging from construction funds for vocational facilities in Appalachia to the support of existing vocational programs.

- Education of the Handicapped (P.L. 94-142) - Since the enactment of the Education For All Handicapped Children Act in 1975, the federal government has been involved in funding special education at all levels of the educational process by providing funds to school districts and to departments of education for the direct support of special education activities. The primary purpose of the act is to provide a free and appropriate education in the least restrictive environment for all handicapped children. Types of programs funded include basic assistance, demonstration programs, resource centers, personnel training and other miscellaneous services.

Where We Stand Now

From no mention of education in the US Constitution, we now have a US Department of Education. The Ohio Department of Education has a federal programs section.

Federal and State mandates, often unfunded, have rendered the cherished "local control of education" more a myth than a reality. Though local school boards are free to decide local education policies in limited areas, one of their major tasks is to assure that the local district is in compliance with state and federal laws and mandates.

There may be no school system or university in America which is willing to forgo available state and federal financial support and, in return, will follow state and federal requirement in order to receive the money.

Many districts have Federal Assistance coordinators to locally manage federal programs. The opportunities presented by these programs, especially for poor districts, is so great that some administrator in the district must be devoting at least part-time to this area. These individuals, in addition to knowing the rules and managing the paperwork, stay current with developments in the field. They are always on the lookout for federal dollars which may help their districts.

School Budget

Schools are everyone's business. It is proper that this should be so. Schools spend tax dollars which are collected from almost everyone in some form or another, be it a sales or income tax, which goes for state support of education, or a property tax or income tax which provides local support.

The school budget year coincides with the school fiscal year, which runs from July 1 to June 30. The fiscal year takes its name from the calendar year in the second half of the fiscal year. A fiscal year running from July 1, 2021 to June 30, 2022 is the 2022 fiscal year (FY 22).

In January of each year, usually at the organizational meeting, each school district begins preparing for the upcoming fiscal year by adopting what is commonly called an "asking budget." This document is due to the County Budget Commission no later than January 20th. A public hearing on the budget is held immediately preceding the meeting where the budget is to be adopted, which is seldom attended by any member of the public.

Many districts inflate this budget to the point where it is of little or no value as an indicator of that district's finances. Since the law provides that school districts can receive no more income in the next calendar year than they asked for in the previous asking budget, they ask for far more than they can possibly receive. If they ask for less than they can receive, the school tax rate will be reduced to bring income in line with what was requested in the asking budget.

The document approved by the board of education sometime during the July-September period (no later than September 30th), though commonly thought of as a budget, is officially known as a "permanent appropriations resolution." It provides as accurate a picture of school income and expenses as can be estimated. School districts often adopt a temporary appropriation resolution by June 30th for the period of July to September, while the permanent budget for the school year is developed.

The law wisely sets the deadline for approving this important document for after the start of the school year. This gives each district the opportunity to see its actual enrollment and determine staffing levels and to build these costs into the appropriations resolution.

School districts have different fund accounts for different purposes. This is to avoid the confusion that would result if all school financial transactions were mixed in the same account. For example, there is a lunchroom fund, a bond retirement fund, several federal fund accounts, a general fund and others.

The day-by-day expenses of the school district are paid from an account called the GENERAL FUND, by far the biggest account which the district has. The general fund account is the only one over which the district has much control. The others are generally "earmarked" for specific purposes so that the district has little choice in how the funds will be managed or spent. For these reasons, when we write of the school budget, we are really writing about the school general fund account.

The income and expenses of the school district are shown through line items in the appropriations resolution, all coded according to the Uniform School Accounting System, which is explained in a later chapter of this book.

District finances can be closely tracked through monthly financial reports which the Treasurer may present in the monthly board agenda. During the fiscal year detailed financial reports must be filed by the Treasurer with the County Auditor, the State Auditor and the Ohio Department of Education. Included are the five year financial forecast, required by HB 412, which is filed with the Ohio Department of Education twice a year, by October 31 and May 31 of each year.

The State Auditor conducts a thorough audit of all school financial transactions on a yearly basis to determine that each transaction was lawful and bills the local district for this service. Districts may now hire private firms to do this audit.

The Five Year Forecast has become a primary financial planning tool and indicator for public schools in Ohio. Financial institutions analyze the five year forecast for financing and bond ratings of the district, while the board of education utilizes the forecast as a long term spending and levy plan for the district. The five year forecast reports on the general operations of the district and includes detailed assumption notes that are also required by the Ohio Department of Education and HB 412. One must realize that the five year forecast is based on projections of the future. However, the five year forecast provides a snapshot of the financial direction of the school district. You can obtain a copy of the five year forecast and forecast assumption notes on the ODE website, school website, or from the district treasurer.

One of these documents, called the Comprehensive Annual Financial Report (CAFR), gives the best overall view of the school district. It contains much more data than are contained in the annual appropriations resolution. The CAFR is due before December 31 and covers the previous fiscal year, which ends June 30. The financial notes and disclosures in the CAFR report or audited financial statements can provide a great insight on school district finances. Also, the management and discussion sections of the CAFR or audited financial statements can provide details on current operations and specific financial events of the school district.

You can obtain a copy of your school district CAFR and the Annual Appropriations Resolution by requesting one from the district treasurer or on the State of Ohio Auditors Office website audit search webpage.

Where does the money come from?

The state of Ohio and the local school district provide about equal funding for the average Ohio school district budget, 42% each. The Federal share is 7% and "other" sources account for 9% . There is an "other" category. It includes such items as student fees, tuition, rental of school facilities, sale of property and other small accounts. Districts with skillful investment programs, and particularly those with large unencumbered financial balances, may earn significant interest income. For most districts, however, the "other" category will not be a large part of the budget.

Where does the money go?

A school system is essentially a service organization. As such, most of its expenses are for salaries to pay the people who perform the services.

Between 80% and 85% of all funds in a typical school budget are set aside to pay salaries and salary-related costs. This supports all the people who work for the schools - teachers, administrators, specialists, custodians, bus drivers, maintenance workers and others.

With just this personnel cost percentage alone, one can gain a fairly accurate view of the fiscal health of the school district. If the personnel allocation is near 80%, the district is in good fiscal health. There will be money available for a broad range of school activities. If the figure is near 85%, the district is probably making cutbacks and headed for the ballot.

Total School Budget

OTHER

PERSONNEL
80%-85%

The cost of a school employee goes beyond salary only. Other salary-related costs, such as retirement, sick leave, hospitalization and life insurance, will add 25% or more to the bill. Below is an example of what a typical teacher will cost a board of education.

Salary – average district teacher salary FY 20*	$83,004
Health insurance- Basic, prescription drug, dental, vision	
Board pays 90%, teacher pays 10%	$26,663
Single -	$10,026
Retirement – board pays 14% of salary to STRS,	$11,621
Substitutes – sick leave, personal leave, in-service	$ 11,190
Medicare-1.45%	$1,204
Life Insurance - $50,000, 10.6 cents/thousand	$64
Workers Compensation- 1% of salary	$332

TOTAL COST $124,077

Note: These data for illustration purposes only. Salary and fringe benefit packages vary widely and are negotiated locally. Some parts of the package, such as health insurance, have shown increases at far higher rates than salary and will drive average costs up. Fringe benefits are generally not taxed and have a greater value to the employee than an equivalent dollar amount placed in salary.

In the remaining 15% to 20% of the budget not allocated to salaries are found many items which the schools must buy in order to stay in operation. They include such things are repairs to school buildings and equipment, electricity, telephone, water, insurance and other similar items. Also in this portion of the budget will be found money for such critical needs as school supplies, library books, textbooks, equipment, transportation and items of a similar nature.

There is very little flexibility in the school budget. After personnel and fixed charges are paid, the board has a very small percentage of the budget which it can allocate in a discretionary fashion.

Thanks to Scott Snyder, Treasurer, Mayfield City Schools, For sample district salary data.

How Personnel Costs are Paid by the Board

The majority of personnel costs are for paying teachers and others who may be on the teacher salary schedule, such as nurses. These are the people who deliver most of the educational services that schools exist to provide. Most other personal costs are for support people; such as bus drivers, who transport the students to and from school; custodians who keep the buildings clean; administrators who structure the school environment and deal with many people and problems, all intended to help the teacher be more effective.

Let us take the structure for paying teachers as our example.

Virtually every public school system in the country pays teachers the same way, with a salary grid. See pg 62 for the actual 2018 teacher salary grid for a northeast Ohio school district. This grid has to meet certain state requirements, but it is basically a local school district document, negotiated between the local school board and the local chapter of a teacher's association which represents the certified employees of that school district.

There are three ways that teachers are paid through this grid.

1. The salary numbers on the grid are negotiated, probably once every three years. When this negotiation takes place, typically most or all the numbers are increased by a small percentage, perhaps 2% or 3%. This number is important since it affects the entire grid. Factors such as inflation or the contracts of nearby school districts will figure prominently in the negotiations. Under this system, assuming a normal economy, everyone on the grid receives an annual increase in salary.

2. Moving across the grid by taking university graduate courses or earning advanced degrees. The wise teacher does this as quickly as possible. The salary increase usually kicks in at the start of the school year after the credits or degrees are earned. The teacher will continue to receive the raise each year for as long as that person is on the salary grid. Since retirement in Ohio is based on the average of the best 5 years of earnings, the retired teacher will continue to receive the benefit of that salary increase for life. Taking a summer or evenings to attend graduate school to improve teaching skills and being paid to do so every year for perhaps 50 years is a good return on investment.

3. Longevity increases. The teacher moves up the grid with each year of experience and receives an increase in salary, typically 3% or 4%. Teachers at the top of the experience grid, 14 years in the case of the example, then may receive longevity increases as they no longer are eligible for increments.

The grid is deliberately top weighted. Associations like to see a 2-1 ratio or more, with teachers are the top making twice as much as beginners. Pay your dues and stick it out and the salary picture brightens quickly.

There is very little teacher turnover in most school districts. An individual who retires after 30 years of service will have spent most of that time (16 of the 30 years) at the top of the salary grid. Probably the majority of teachers in most school districts are at the top of the salary grid.

The salary grid may be a factor in employment decisions, making it difficult for much more expensive, experienced teachers to change districts.

Teacher's Salary Schedule
Effective 2021/22 School Year

Years Experience	BA	150 HRS OR BA+9	BA+18	BA+27	MA	MA+9	MA+18	MA+27	DR OR MA+60
0	46,967	47,704	48,460	49,188	49,995	52,837	55,710	58,554	61,467
1	49,387	50,305	51,246	52,158	53,134	55,986	58,868	61,715	64,635
2	51,804	52,908	54,026	55,126	56,270	59,136	62,026	64,881	67,807
3	54,219	55,511	56,811	58,099	59,412	62,282	65,181	68,040	70,972
4	56,638	58,112	59,591	61,065	62,549	65,432	68,333	71,201	74,143
5	59,055	60,714	62,376	64,037	65,689	68,577	71,489	74,366	77,314
6	61,475	63,317	65,162	67,003	68,825	71,727	74,646	77,528	80,483
7	63,888	665,913	67,941	69,975	71,970	74,876	77,801	80,682	83,653
8	66,309	68,516	70,728	72,945	75,105	78,020	80,955	83,856	86,818
9	68,728	71,116	73,513	75,914	78,244	81,173	84,113	87,016	89,990
10	71,146	73,719	76,294	78,882	81,379	84,321	87,271	90,180	93,161
11	73,557	76,320	79,080	81,853	84,517	87,466	90,421	93,341	96,332
12	75,979	78,924	81,857	84,824	87,657	90,614	93,576	96,505	99,496
13	78,398	81,825	84,644	87,790	90,798	93,765	96,734	99,668	102,664
14	-	-	-	-	93,933	96,911	99,889	102,827	105,834

Teachers with 15 years or more of service recognized for salary schedule placement will receive an additional $2,581. Teachers with 20 years or more of service recognized for salary schedule placement will receive an additional $2,942. Teachers with 25 years or more of service recognized for salary schedule placement will receive an additional $3,303.

All amounts are received annually and payable with the last pay in June. The Federal withholding tax for the additional payments will be calculated based on the current year's Internal Revenue Service publication, Circular E, Employers Tax Guide.

Sick Leave, Personal Leave, Faculty Assignment

School employees, including teachers, are entitled by law to 15 days of sick leave per year. Sick leave accumulates at the rate of 1 ¼ day per month. The law determines when the sick leave is earned, not when it is used. Sick leave not used in any given year is accumulated. If a teacher has a serious illness or is entitled to a leave extending more than 15 days per year, such as for pregnancy, accumulated sick leave can then be used. It is common, through local negotiations, for these accumulated days not used, or a portion or percentage of them, be paid to the employee upon qualified retirement, at the daily rate the teacher is earning at the time of retirement. For a dedicated teacher who enjoys good health, the amount awarded as retirement severance pay is a welcome financial reward at the end of a long career of service in education.

In addition, districts negotiate personal leave days, typically 3. The number and the reasons these days may be used are a matter for local negotiation. If these days are not allowed to accumulate, there exists and incentive for them to be used each year. Both sick and personal leave amount to 18 days per year, almost 10% of the total 185 day work year.

Another personnel cost has to do with teacher assignment. The typical high school day will have 8 periods with 5 teaching period assignments. Districts, needing someone to handle an important but time consuming co-curricular assignment, such as the student yearbook or newspaper, may release a teacher from one class assignment, reducing the teaching load to handle the co-curricular assignment during the school day. It appears that there is no cost since no staff is added. However, the math shows a different picture. If a high school teacher earns the mean $64,935 per year and works 8 periods, the cost is $8,117 per year per period. If the salary is divided by the 5 teaching periods, the teacher earns $12,907 per teaching period per year. Taking the teacher out of the classroom for whatever reason to perform other duties may be necessary but it is a high cost practice.

Educator Retirement in Ohio

There are 5 public employee retirement systems in Ohio, two of which serve public school districts. They are the State Teacher Retirement System (STRS) which serves certificated employees (teachers, administrators, counselors etc) and the School Employee Retirement System (SERS) which serves all other school employees (bus drivers, custodians, cafeteria staff etc).

Employees and their employing boards make contributions to the retirement system during the working lifetime of the employee. For STRS the educator contributes 14% of salary and the employing board contributes 14%. SERS employee share remains at 10%.

When an employee retires, that person, and the employing board, stop making contributions to the retirement system and start drawing benefits. These after retirement benefits are paid by the retirement system from 3 sources: (1) the contributions which the employee has made to the system, (2) the contribution which the employing board has made to the system and (3) investment income which the retirement system receives from investing the contributions made by the employees and boards. *Once an educator retires in Ohio, no additional tax dollars are used to fund the retirement benefits.*

The local district budget

Definition: A school district budget is a yearly financial plan which funds the school program the district residents desire for their children and are willing to pay for.

Financial prediction

The yearly budget (appropriations resolution) is intended to predict the financial details of district operations for the upcoming year. Because the credibility and competence of school leaders is at risk in this process, the reader should understand the difficulty of making financial predictions in school finance.

There are literally hundreds of sources of income and expenses which must be projected in order to build a school budget. Many of these sources are outside the control of the district.

On the **expense side** of the ledger, for example, if liability insurance takes a big jump because of a State Supreme Court decision (and it has), there is no way district officials could have predicted this. Health care costs, court decisions, a change in special education regulations, unfunded mandates such as the No Child Left Behind Act, the list of unpredictable expenses could go on extensively.

On the **income side**, there are many areas difficult, if not impossible, to predict accurately.

The district and its leaders suffer if the expected income needed to pay the bills does not materialize. The pain can be even worse if the district receives more income than expected. This is especially true if a district recently failed a levy which the board of education said was badly needed. Perhaps they just concluded negotiations with district unions and held to a strict budget line. "LOCAL SCHOOLS RECEIVE FINANCIAL WINDFALL" is not a newspaper headline district people want to see under those circumstances.

How can the district receive MORE money than expected? The County Auditor may underestimate the income a district will receive.

The Auditor is motivated to be conservative in estimating income. The Auditor does not want to be blamed for a budget shortfall.

School officials do work to make the budget as accurate as possible. They pay attention to local factors that might affect the budget, such as changes in property valuation, new housing developments or factory closings. They follow legislative developments at the state level as monitored by the various state education associations. They keep track of financial information from past years in order to create income and expense trend lines for all areas of income and expenditures.

If financial circumstances change during the fiscal year, the board can file an amended appropriations resolution to **incorporate the change**.

It is also important for school officials to educate district citizens about the factors explained above.

Building the budget

Many districts are so starved for funds that all they can do is survive financially from year to year. In districts like this the objective will be to hold expenditure increases for the next year in all line items to about the rate of inflation. An attempt will then be made to take into account special circumstances in the income and expenditure items where deviations from the inflation number are expected. These are worked into the budget. The final step will be to take a look at the sum of all expense and income items. Invariably the expense items will be larger. Cuts are then made based upon district priorities as seen by the budget builders until the budget is balanced.

In more fortunate districts the budget emerges from the STRATEGIC PLAN. These districts usually involve students, staff members and residents in an organized process to answer questions like "Where do we want this district to go? What things are most important to accomplish? How can we best spend money to improve this district?"

From the strategic plan will come specific tactics, action steps which must be taken to reach the stated goals. In the budgeting process, funding these action steps is given a high priority. In these districts the budget is used to give DIRECTION to the district.

What about "fat" in the school budget?

When it comes time to vote another tax increase for schools, and this happens every few years in Ohio, there is a frequent charge that the schools do not really need the additional money. The complainant usually goes on to suggest that the schools could easily operate without additional funds if they would eliminate frills, waste and inefficiency. The complainant may even go on to point out an example or two where the schools are buying services or materials which he or she considers unnecessary.

The real situation, as shown in the section above, is that the school budget does not have much flexibility. Since the great bulk of school funds go for personnel, the only way any significant reduction in the school budget can be made is to reduce the number of people who work for the schools. Each employee is hired to perform some job. The elimination of any position eliminates the service which that person provides for the schools. Almost without exception, reducing personnel reduces the quality of education which a district provides for its students.

Only 15% to 20% of the school budget is allocated to the non-salary area. A large percentage of this money is applied to items, such as electricity and heat, which are needed just to keep the schools open. What remains after these bills are paid, perhaps 5% of the total budget is allocated to those items which a school system could do without for short emergency periods only.

They include such items as field trips, pupil transportation not required by state law, athletics, and extra-curricular activities for students and others.

When contemplating reductions in the school budget such as those listed above, here are several important considerations:

• Is the item to be eliminated really a reduction in expenditures or just a postponement? For example, items such as buses and equipment simply wear out. The district that postpones these purchases for several years may find itself playing an expensive game of catch-up in order to struggle back to the previous level of operations.

• How many dollars in state funds will the district have to give up to save one dollar of local funds? For example, in the area of transportation or vocational and special education, the state reimburses most local districts for a large part of their costs. The district which eliminates them not only eliminates large items of expenditures but also cuts off state subsidies which are an item of income.

• Are the items required by federal law, state law or are they necessary to meet state standards? The district which does not meet standards in any area, be it class size or number of books per pupil in the library, risks losing state foundation support.

There are many federal laws, such as Title IX, involving equal treatment of the sexes, which districts are required to follow if they wish to receive federal funds.

Many people who complain about frills and waste really are disagreeing with the spending priorities of the schools. If they had their way, they would spend the money differently. The athletic booster club member may think the speech and hearing therapist is a frill. The parents of the child with a speech disorder think the therapist is vital but, since they live next to the school, may think the district spends too much on busing. The parents who live on a narrow road think that busing is a necessary safety item for their first grader but may think that the athletic program is a waste of money.

When an item of expenditure is criticized, school officials must consider it fairly in light of the needs of the whole district. One person's frill is another's necessity.

When the inflexibility of the school budget and the implications of cuts in the budget are fully realized by the people, necessary funds are generally voted for the schools.

Why Do Schools Keep Asking For More Money?

Individual states have set up different mechanisms to control increases in public school costs. There are three common systems. In Pennsylvania, for example, the school board sets the budget and control resides in the citizen ability to elect school board members. In New York the community initially votes on the entire budget, sometimes at a town meeting, up or down. If the initial budget fails, the board proposes to cut the same kind of services that boards in Ohio bring forth, such as transportation and athletics and the community votes on those items. In Ohio, the Legislature has provided a long list of ballot opportunities for school boards to raise revenue.

According to data gathered by the Ohio School Boards Association, there were 73 school issues on the ballot with 50 issues passing in May of 2021 (a 68% passage rate). However, only 9 of 25 new school tax issues were approved (a 36% passage rate). New tax issues continue to be a challenge for Ohio public school districts as taxpayers continue to reject additional taxes for current operating expenses. The previous ballot in November of 2020 had 113 issues on the ballot, a substantial decrease from the 151 ballots in November of 2016.

Why are there so many local school issues on the ballot in Ohio? In simplest terms, restrictions on school income growth caused by HB 920 combined with increasing costs, many of which are outside the control of local school officials, force local boards of education to place these issues on the ballot to meet expenses.

School districts have only four basic ways to receive increased income:
• additional taxable property, either new construction or increased tangible personal property, is added to the school district tax duplicate.
• the General Assembly increases state aid for schools.
• reassessment and updates produce a small amount of additional income from inside mills.
• the school district passes a local financial issue.

Although there are notable exceptions, passing local financial issues is the only way most school districts can secure enough additional funds to meet expenses. When you think about it, what else but their responsibility to the education of the children of the community would cause a local board of education to choose to suffer the ire and upset which these local levies commonly cause?

If you understand the chart on the front and back cover of this book, you understand the problem. A typical pattern (referring to the chart) is for a district to pass a levy to meet increasing costs. School income exceeds expenses in the first year after the levy. Money not needed for operations that year is set aside and carried over to the next year. You can see this amount as an "unencumbered balance" in the summary page of the district appropriations resolution. In the second year income and expenses are about equal. By the third year expenses exceed income and the money set aside in the first year is used to meet current expenses. Since the district is now in a deficit spending situation, they must go on the ballot again for another operating issue to pay expenses and the pattern continues.

What are some factors which keep driving up school expenses?

Legal requirements and other unfunded mandates

In America we expect our schools, as government agencies, to be the models which bridge the gap between the rhetoric and the reality of America's ideals. Various courts, agencies and levels of government have the ability to require schools to take certain actions in the interest of fairness, equity or safety, but have no obligations to provide the funds to pay for these actions.

The shortcut term for this situation is "unfunded mandates." Unfunded mandates are distressing to school officials because local spending priorities are superceded by the mandates. School district officials and taxpayers allocate their available funds in ways which they believe produce the best educational return for the money. With unfunded mandates, some authority outside the school district imposes its spending priority upon the local school district, its budget and its taxpayers. In effect they are saying, "You will spend your available money to accomplish what we tell you to do and then spend what is left according to your local priorities." Since there is then not enough money left to meet the local needs, the unfunded mandates often force local school authorities to ask their taxpayers for additional funds.

Here are some examples of this situation:

Federal law imposes a substantial list of mandates on local school. The massive (900+ pages) *No Child Left Behind Act of 2001* represents the biggest unfunded mandate for local schools in history. A long list of federal laws is aimed at assuring fair treatment for all people. The "fair treatment" principle requires that special classes and services be provided for all youngsters with handicaps. Elevators, ramps, special rest rooms, specially equipped buses and fire warning systems may be required in buildings to make them accessible and safe for the handicapped.

Sexual harassment in any form is illegal.

In a 1999 Supreme Court case, Aurelia Davis v. Monroe County School Board, the Court found school districts liable in certain circumstances if students sexually harass each other. Justice Kennedy, dissenting, wrote, "We can be assured that like suits will follow - which in cost and number, will impose serious financial burdens on local school districts, the taxpayers who support them and the children they serve."

Employment practices may have to be expanded to remove all vestiges of discrimination in hiring.

Both sexes must be treated equally. Additional coaches and facilities may have to be provided to assure that girls and boys receive equal treatment.

Extensive evaluation, disciplinary and termination procedures are required to be certain every school employee's rights are protected.

Proper procedures are required before students can be suspended or expelled, in order to protect their right to an education.

In many instances the function of the school is expanded by the General Assembly. Recent actions include creation of a statewide Education Management Information System (EMIS). School districts are now mandated to collect an incredible amount of detailed information about 27 different areas of school operations. They must then transmit the information by computer to the Ohio Department of Education and make copies of their report available to the general public.

Probably the greatest source of unfunded mandates is the State Legislature. As the body responsible for public elementary and secondary education in Ohio, the Legislature is constantly looking for, and imposing, mandates designed to improve school performance - without being responsible for the tax increases to fund the improvement effort.

State courts place new mandates on schools. In recent years the Ohio Supreme Court has found that nurses and tutors must be paid as teachers, adding millions of dollars to school district salary costs.

Districts must spend whatever funds that are required to meet inspection standards of the many agencies which have jurisdiction over various aspects of school operations. School buses, building construction, boilers, asbestos removal and fire safety are a few such areas which receive close inspection.

The inspecting agency expects its standards to be fully met in schools and does not consider the financial condition of the school district when making its findings. The schools must meet the standards to remain in business, no matter the cost. If an inspection shows that your school district's underground gas tank has been leaking and it costs $100,000 to dig up and dispose of the contaminated soil and to fully repair the situation, your district has no choice but to spend the money.

Inflation

Though the rate of inflation has been low by historic standards in recent years, inflation is still a big factor in the economic life of the nation. Schools, as service organizations, are particularly vulnerable to the ravages of inflation. Most of the school budget goes to pay salaries and fringe benefits. These are the traditional leaders in the upward spiral of inflation. In addition to the salary factor, inflation drives up the cost of everything the schools buy in the way of supplies, equipment, and materials, health care for employees and energy needs.

Although most citizens are aware that they must receive a salary increase every year to keep up with inflation, few graciously accept the fact that they must pay more for the goods and services they receive because every dollar they pay with is worth less.

Because of inflation, schools must have more tax dollars just to maintain their current levels of services.

Expanded services

The function of the school in American society is constantly expanding. Schools are under constant pressure from their publics to expand services. All-day kindergarten, pre-school, daycare, more extra-curricular opportunities, HIV education, expanded bus service and lunch programs are among the areas of current demand. In some cases, the changing nature of families requires that schools perform services for children, which traditional families - a rapidly diminishing segment of our population - used to perform.

Services for special students

In 1975 Congress passed Public Law 94-142 (Education of All Handicapped Children Act), now codified as IDEA (Individuals with Disabilities Education Act).

The heart of IDEA is the language that "all handicapped students shall receive a free, appropriate public education in the least restrictive environment".

Since the law was passed, the cost of service to special populations has become to the school budget what the cost of health care has become to the federal and state budgets – expanding rapidly and a threat to the overall budget with no workable plan in place to slow or check the expansion.

According to ESC 50, June of 2015, "About 13 percent of all public school students receive special educational services and state spending for these student is rising." In FY 2014 IDEA federal funding covered only 16 percent of the estimated excess cost of educating children with disabilities. It was 33% six years earlier. The shortfall must be covered by states and local school districts. These are called unfunded mandates. One level of government, a court or legislature, says "This is what you must do." Their concern is justice, not cost. Paying to render the justice falls on the actual service provider, usually local boards of education.

There are a number of forces affecting special education costs:

Expansion of special education categories – The latest addition to the list of disabilities are attention deficit disorder (ADD) and attention deficit/hyperactivity disorder (ADHD). These disabilities are difficult to diagnose. Many students, primarily boys, in the school setting have the symptoms to a more or less degree. A physician is required to diagnose if the symptoms are severe enough to be called disabilities.

Legal opinions – Over time schools have learned that it is difficult to win a special education court case. Courts have decided that a student does not have to benefit from educational services to receive them, that parents can place their children in special private schools and have the school district pay, that cost is not a factor in determining if students can receive special services, that the school will pay the fees for both attorneys and that parents can litigate special education cases without an attorney. It is common for school districts to approve disability service requests rather than going to the expense of contesting them, with a good chance of not being successful. Courts have decided that a special student:

*does not have to benefit from educational services to receive them (Timothy W. v. Rochester, New Hampshire School District, 1989).

* is entitled to an individual educational plan (IEP), (Board of Education v. Rowley, 1982) and that the IEP is legally enforceable.

ᐧ should be educated in the least restricted environment, which means mainstreaming unless the district can show that a segregated facility would offer superior educational services (Roncker v. Walter, 1983)

* may be placed by the parents in a private school with the school district paying the costs if a court determines that the district IEP is inappropriate (Burlington v. Department of Education, Massachusetts, 1985) and may do so without the child ever attending a public school (Forest Grove School District v. T.A., 2009). There are now 90,000 children so enrolled. In the T.A. case, from Oregon, tuition is $62,400 per year in the residential School of the parents' choice.

*is entitled to catherization and continuous nursing services as "related services" (Irving Independent School District v. tarto, 1984,

Cedar Rapids Community School District v. Garrett F., 1999, and Endew v. Douglas County, 2017)

The school district may be liable for the legal fees of parents, as well as paying its own, under the "prevailing party" rule (Public law 99- 372). Courts commonly find some way to award attorney fees to the parents, perhaps feeling that a school district with its resources is better able to pay the fees than the parents of a handicapped child. There are now many attorneys specializing in IDEA litigation.

Benefits of the Services – In the school environment, many benefit from special services for students with disabilities. Regular teachers appreciate the help (but may not appreciate mainstreaming), the parents want the individual or special attention for their child, school officials want happy parents, service providers want the jobs. The dynamic is in favor of classifying students as having special needs.
(Please see Endew v. Douglas County, p84).

Improved benefits for school personnel

For many years school employees accepted relatively low salaries and fringe benefits as part of their lives. This is no longer true. Today school employees have demanded, and received, salaries and benefits more in line with their training and contribution to society.

Higher salaries obviously cost school districts more money but the increase in the cost of fringe benefits, especially health care has been very large in past decades. Since fringe benefits like health care are tax free and their cost is not generally publicized, school boards and staff associations have sometimes preferred them to increases in salary.

However, school employees have also benefited by a restructuring of their duties. Such things as smaller class sizes, more professional planning time and release from routine clerical duties have required schools to hire more personnel to perform duties previously handled by teachers. It is also important to note that most school districts have approximately one non-certified employee for every teacher. These school workers - classroom aides, custodians, secretaries, bus drivers, cafeteria workers and others - perform a valuable service for the schools and wish to be compensated accordingly.

Technology

Technology has increased school costs. Technology is part of life today. Almost all students will use expensive and complex machines in their jobs or at home. In order to use the technology, schools have to buy it, maintain it, and replace it when it becomes obsolete. Schools can't train students on manual typewriters when the world is using computers. That's not education for real life.

Substitute teacher costs

The US department of education reports that the average teacher is absent 9.4 days of the 180 day school year.

Your local school administrators will verify that the use of substitute teachers has risen dramatically in recent years.

In addition to sick leave, personal leave, family leave and maternity leave, the drive for educational excellence has increased the use of substitute teachers. More in-service for teachers is required to improve performance. State and federally mandated proficiency testing requirements now drive the local school curriculum. Curriculum alignment, curriculum mapping and instructional improvement efforts are major initiatives in most districts. These activities typically take place during the school day and require the use of substitute teachers. It would be reasonable to conclude that the daily rate of substitute teachers will increase in order to help alleviate shortages. Districts may add permanent substitutes to the payroll, paying them on a teacher salary schedule.

If you want to come up with a disturbing thought, consider that an important item which correlates 1-1 with student learning is time on task. Then consider the days in the school year, calculate how many days the teacher can be absent with pay, how many days the student is absent, days where items such as holidays lead to other than academic learning; pep rallies, interruptions over the school PA system, the entire culture of our school environment which makes it such a rich growing experience for young people and then ask yourself, "What of the above are we going to take away to provide more time on task?"

Community (charter) schools, electronic schools, vouchers

Ohio legislature has provided well for alternatives to public schools. These schools receive about the state basic aid amount per pupil as public schools. They also receive supplemental aid, the home district's poverty based assistance funds, parity aid, etc.

According to the Ohio Legislative Service commission, transfers of state aid from public schools to community and STEM schools amounted to about $940 million in FY 2016. Bonus payment to these schools amounted to $2.6 million in FY 2016.

The apparent intention of the legislature is to assure that any money coming from the state to the local district to educate a student will be deducted from that district's state aid and given to the school in which the student is actually enrolled. In addition, the law provides that any local money which is part of the state basic aid amount will also be deducted from the state aid of the public school and given to the alternative school.

Should the situation exist that the deduction from the resident district does not exceed the total amount of state aid received by the district, including rollback and homestead payments, the contention of alternative schools advocates is that no local money is transferred to community schools. By law, the amount deducted from a district cannot exceed the total state aid received by the district. It is true that the money follows the students, but also true that the transfer of one or two students per classroom to community schools results in a minimal reduction in public schools costs, not nearly as much as is taken away from the public school and sent to the community school.

The financial opportunities for profit which are made available by the law have drawn private sector entrepreneurial activity.

E-schools provide a student with a computer, DSL line, modem and online instruction. They have no cost for school buildings and grounds, transportation, food service, co-curricular activities, schools used as community centers, or support and special services. Yet they receive funding according to the same basic formula as public schools which do provide all these things.

According to a recent article in the Cleveland Plain Dealer, 31% of charter schools are operated for -profit. Fifty three percent of the state money going to charter schools went to for-profit schools. Entrepreneurs have learned how to navigate the system, to the detriment of public school funding.

The pioneer operator of charter schools in Ohio is White Hat Management, an Akron based company owned by entrepreneur David Brennan. White Hat has had mixed success and a troubled legal history. It once enrolled about 10,000 students, a number now greatly diminished. White Hat has sold 12 elementary charter school contracts to Pansophic Learning, which also runs the Ohio Virtual Academy, making it Ohio's largest charter school operator. In 2006 a group of 10 charter schools sued White Hat Management in an attempt to negate a signed contract regarding ownership of materials and equipment (see pg 91.) That legal attempt failed, but the group of schools hired Cambridge Educational Group to manage the ten schools. White Hat and Cambridge are now operating concurrently.

There are some truly non-profit charter and E-schools which operate in partnership with public schools. Other "non-profit" schools are not that at all. The same entity that owns the non-profit school also owns the company which supplies the school. By selling an $800 computer to the non-profit school for $8,000, the school ends the year drained of all money and is non-profit, but the supplier, who is the same person, does very well.

On October 25, 2006 the Ohio Supreme Court approved the Charter School Law.

Choice Scholarships (vouchers) are designed to free the student from the requirement that all students must attend the public school which serves their residential address. The vouchers generally are available to students who attend failing schools, low income students in the Cleveland district and special education students throughout Ohio. HB 153 has significantly expanded the voucher program, both in numbers of scholarships available to students and by new provisions in law which expand the numbers and categories of students who are eligible for vouchers.

Property tax abatements

The business property tax abatement program in Ohio is extensive. Local municipalities can grant the elimination of all or a partial elimination (abatement) of real estate taxes in order to attract new businesses into the community. The revenue from business income taxes can often outweigh real estate tax revenue collected by municipalities due to the much lower millage that a municipality collects in comparison to school districts. As a result, local municipalities are willing to forgo small real estate revenue streams in order to pick up great increases in income tax due to new payroll from a business moving into the jurisdiction. In the meantime, Ohio school districts suffer from diluted collection due to partial abatement or, even worse, a full abatement. Local municipalities can grant up to a 75% abatement without the permission of the school district.

The general concept is that if businesses are exempt from property taxes for a number of years, that exemption will draw new construction and jobs to specified areas. Some may argue that the school districts will see an increase in tax revenue after the abatements expire and the decision to abate can become very political in the community.

Most local property taxes go to schools. Jobs provide increased income tax revenue for those municipalities granting the abatements. Thus we have a situation where municipalities can give away tax money which would be coming to schools in order to gain income tax revenue for the municipalities. The amount of abatements for the State is measured in billions of dollars, so one can imagine the magnitude of the abatements.

Property tax exemptions

Governmental agencies, charities, churches, private schools and colleges all receive tax exemptions. The second biggest beneficiary of tax exemptions, after schools, are businesses. In the last 15 years the value of business tax exempt property has increased by 480% in Ohio. Research on tax exemptions published in the April 10, 2002 edition of the Akron Beacon Journal and written by Doug Oplinger and Dennis Willard lead off with the sentence "In Ohio, businesses now get more property tax breaks than God." Tangible personal property used in business is no longer taxed in Ohio.

Tax exemptions are controversial in some quarters. For example, in Cuyahoga County the Cleveland Clinic owns 4.5% of the real estate in the city. It has tax exempt status. They are obligated to pay nothing to support the schools. They protect this tax exempt status with vigor, explaining that they perform significant charitable services for the community.

Exempt property in the State of Ohio is also measured in the billions, impacting the tax revenue of school districts. Since the local property tax is the main source of revenue for schools, someone in the district, usually the Treasurer, has to be paying attention to the property tax base at all times to avoid surprises, especially unpleasant ones. For example, property must come on to the tax duplicate and the property tax paid before an exemption is applied for. If an appeal is filed, resolution may take some time. If the appeal is granted, the district may be faced with granting a refund. Districts must plan accordingly for property tax exemptions since the property value has to come onto the tax duplicate prior to the State granting the exemption. For some Districts, this may be a fast process within the current tax year yielding no problems with tax revenue projections. However, some businesses and entities may appeal for the tax exemptions through a process that may occur over multiple years. In the meantime, the entity may pay the property taxes during the appeal process, yielding a potential refund due if the exemption is ultimately approved by the State. School districts should keep a pulse on new construction or businesses that may eventually be granted an exemption. This is often accomplished with the expertise of legal counsel that specializes in tax board of revisions and tax property valuation cases on behalf of the district.

Current Agricultural Use Value

ORC 5713 requires county auditors, upon application from landowners, to assess qualified agricultural property according to its current agricultural use value (CAUV) instead of at its "highest and best" use value. The land must be used exclusively for agriculture. Over 16.1 million acres of Ohio land is so assessed, giving this land an assessed value, about half of the "highest and best use" value. Thus about 10 billion of assessed value is lost to schools and other local governments.

HB 49 broadened and liberalized CAUV deductions. The net result will be either a shift of the property tax burden to residential property or a decrease in income for schools.

Note: For an analysis of the interplay of CUV with a shift in the tax burden, HB 920, inside versus outside millage, state share index and state aid see the March 8, 2017 paper by Dr. Howard Fleeter of the Ohio Education Policy Institute, "Analysis of HB 398 & SB 246…"

When local school districts place issues on the ballot, it is common to find them criticized for doing so. This chapter should give the reader a better understanding of why those issues are on the ballot.

Local Voting Decisions

Decisions on local school levies are important. Every school issue has a direct monetary effect upon every property owner or renter in the district. Further, every issue also has a direct effect upon the education of all young people in the school district. Your vote should be carefully considered. Below are some factors which you will want to take into account before making a decision on a school issue.

How to decide "yes" or "no" on school issues

Judge the issues on their own merits - Do not mix up your feelings toward the levy or bond issue with conflicts or dissatisfaction with school policies, procedures or the people who work for the schools. There are many ways of making your feelings on these matters known, from voting against school board members and speaking out at school board meetings to complaining about a school employee to his or her immediate supervisor. You cannot get back at adults who work for the schools by voting against a tax issue which is designed to benefit children.

Get the big picture - More than schools and children are involved in school issues. You should also consider how the passage or failure of the issue will affect such things as community spirit, community growth and even the value of your own home. For example, you may conclude that potential home buyers with children will not want to select a home in a community with poor schools. Decreased property values may cost you much more than the levy would.

Make financial comparisons - Concentrate on the cost per pupil figures between your district and others in the area. If others spend more per pupil, chances are they are buying more and their students are getting more. Your aim is to help provide the kind of education in your district which will give the students at least a fair start as they go out to compete against their neighbors for the good things in life.

Get the facts - Find out what the levy proceeds will be used for, how much the issue will cost you, how its passage will benefit children and what will happen if it fails. Your school officials will be making a great effort to get this information to each citizen. Read the published materials carefully. Call the school office if you have further questions. Remember, it's your money they are asking for.

Beware of rumors - In every school election a good percentage of the people in the community will be against the issue. In general, they oppose the issue simply because they are unwilling to spend the additional money for schools.

However, since this reason is socially unpopular, many people who intend to vote no on the school issue search around for a reason why the schools do not "deserve" the money. They then use this reason with their neighbors and with themselves so they cannot be accused of voting against the welfare of children.

This process of rationalization produces some fantastic rumors and horror stories. Use good judgment when you hear such stories, generally about how schools are wasting large amounts of money, planning to give large salary increases or neglecting their educational duties. Recognize the reasons why these kinds of stories are spread. Better yet, call the administrative offices of your school district for the facts. The staff will be eager to hear from you as this gives them a chance to set the record straight.

Cost, values, priorities - What you value is revealed through what you buy with your money. Every school election should be an occasion for taking stock and reviewing personal priorities. It's time for balancing an expenditure for schools as a means of improving many young lives and helping to provide a new generation of productive citizens against a similar expenditure for something else - perhaps some material thing, entertainment or similar items.

Tax Issues are a Last Resort for School Boards

School boards do not want to ask local residents for more money. They do it because they were elected to provide good schools for the community and this is the only way they can maintain the quality of education in the district for which they are responsible.

School issues require a major time and effort campaign by many of the education minded people in your community. They often face criticism from some residents who question the need for, and the cost of, some areas of school operations. There may even be a counter group whose members work against passage of the school issue. The resistance, which may come in many guises, really comes down to one - they are not willing to pay additional taxes to support good schools.

Residents can be assured that when the school board is willing to undertake all that is required to win a school issue election, they do so out of necessity.

The Courts and School Finance

School law, once a dormant field, has been booming in the past several decades. Integration, student rights, negotiations, due process, special education and school finance have all been the subject of judicial cases, either directly or indirectly affecting the financing of your local schools. The following school finance cases merit your attention.

LEADING CASES

Serrano v. Priest

The major base for the financing of public education in 49 of the 50 states is the local property tax. Hawaii, which has one state school system, is the only exception.

Because the amount of taxable property per student varies among local school districts, there are also variations in tax rates, per pupil expenditures and quality of education. Most districts, of course, fall within the average range on all these factors, but startling differences are not difficult to find.

These disparities have long been emphasized by those calling for greater equalization in school financing; however, the current system is firmly established and resistant to change.

The first successful attack upon the property tax as the major source of school financial support took place in California. In September of 1971 the California State Supreme Court, in the now-famous case of *Serrano v. Priest*, struck a blow against the California method of financing schools. At that time schools in California, as in most of the rest of the nation, were financed by a combination of local property tax proceeds and state aid.

In an eloquent decision which has been quoted around the nation, the California Supreme Court ruled that basing public school financing on the individual district's taxable resources "invidiously discriminates against the poor because it makes the quality of a child's education a function of the wealth of his parents and neighbors."

The court further stated: "As a practical matter, districts with small tax bases simply cannot levy taxes at a rate sufficient to produce the revenue that more affluent districts reap with minimal tax efforts. Affluent districts can have their cake and eat it too; they can provide a high quality education for their children while paying lower taxes. Poor districts, by contrast, have no cake at all."

Finally, in a much quoted dictum, the court ruled, "Education may not be a function of wealth, except the wealth of the state as a whole."

It should be pointed out that the California court did not find that state's method of financing schools to violate the state constitution as happened in New Jersey *(Robinson V. Cahill)*.

Nor was the decision based upon the strict merits of the case. The comments made by the California Supreme Court in Serrano were part of a decision to send the case back to a lower court to be tried on its own merits. The major impact of the Serrano case has been political rather than legal in that is has caused courts and legislatures around the nation to focus upon the legality of unequal educational funding.

Rodriguez v. San Antonio Independent School District

Shortly after the Serrano v. Priest decision was handed down lawsuits quoting the Serrano case were filed in over 30 states. One was filed in Ohio by the Ohio Education Association, which represents most of Ohio's teachers. Within a matter of months the Serrano reasoning was quoted and applied by courts in New Jersey, Minnesota, Wyoming, Arizona and Texas as they, too, ruled in favor of those challenging the present system of financing schools. The Texas case, *Rodriguez*, was handed down by a U.S. District Court. As a federal case it was the first to reach the Supreme Court.

The *Rodriguez* case was based upon the equal protection clause of the Fourteenth Amendment. The Supreme Court had to decide if education was a fundamental right guaranteed by the Constitution, and, if so, whether or not the current method of financing education denied that right to a class of citizens.

For several months the court deliberated this case, in which the U.S. Supreme Court could have declared the school tax and support laws of 49 states illegal. In March of 1973, in a 5-4 decision, the court rejected Rodriguez's complaint and upheld the San Antonio Board of Education. By so doing, the constitutionality of school support schemes primarily dependent upon the property tax, such as that currently in effect in Ohio, was affirmed.

Although the U.S. Supreme Court did not conclude that "the Texas system of financing public education operates to the disadvantage of some suspect class or impinges upon a fundamental right explicitly or implicitly protected by the Constitution," the court by no means endorsed current methods of financing schools.

In this line the court stated, "the need is apparent for reform in tax systems which may well have relied too long and too heavily on the local property tax...but the ultimate solutions must come from the (state) lawmakers and from the democratic pressures of those who elect them."

When the constitutionality of current school financing methods was affirmed in the U.S. Supreme Court, the battle for equalization shifted to state legislatures and courts all over the nation.

Since the 1973 U.S. Supreme Court decision in *Rodriquez*, school finance decisions have been made by the supreme courts of about three quarters of our 50 states.

Some states, Ohio being among them, have had multiple decisions. In this state- by- state review process, virtually every aspect of school funding has been challenged and examined. Major attention has been given to *sources of funding*, especially the heavy reliance on the property tax, and *spending for education*, with a strong attempt to reach consensus on the concepts of *adequacy and equity*. The process has not produced a national consensus about how to fund our public schools.

For a taste of a few of the most important decisions made in other states, look up *Abbott V Burke* and *Robinson V. Cahill* in New Jersey and *Rose v. Council for Better Education* in Kentucky. The multiple *DeRolph* decisions here in Ohio are discussed later in this book.

Endew V. Douglas County

Every word of PL 94-142 has been extensively litigated. On January 11 of 2017 the U.S. Supreme Court handed down a unanimous decision in Endew V. Douglas County answering the question. "What level of the benefit does the law require?" The judges set a new and higher standard of required benefit which has the potential to affect millions of special education students and their school districts. Schools must now offer special education students an IEP (Individual Education Plan) "reasonably calculated" to enable a student "to make progress appropriate in light of the child's circumstances."

There are several ways that schools attempt to meet the requirements of P.L. 94-142 for special students. The first, and least costly, is to offer classes within the school district. For low incidence disabilities, districts band together and build special schools for these students. Transportation and related costs are high, but the hope is that enough students with specific disabilities can be brought together to form a class which will meet their needs. The last level of service, and one which schools generally resist because of the cost, is placement with an outside provider. Some of these schools have yearly tuition in the 6 figures. After Endew, we are sure to see more of these placements.

US Supreme Court - Direction - Alternatives to

Public Schools

Thomas Jefferson is famous for calling for "a wall of separation between church and state." At one time some 39 state constitutions had so called Blaine Amendments, which were primarily designed to prevent public funding of Catholic schools but the concept was generally extended to all non-public schools.

The Supreme Court legal view gradually changed. The strict separation of church and state, based on the first amendment, was once the overriding legal concern. Gradually the Court began giving greater weight to options to public schools that provided increased educational opportunities for students.

The introduction of the Child benefit Theory (Everson V Board of Education- 1947), which holds that public funds could be spent in religious schools if the funds benefitted the child, not the church, was the turning point. In the later cases The Court held that services could be provided on a religious school campus (Agostini V Felton-1997). The court approved the Cleveland School voucher case (Zelman V. Simmons-Harris -2002), allowing scholarships of $2250 awarded to poor students in an underperforming school system to be spent at the school of the parent's choice, The court cited <u>discrimination</u> because the State of Colorado <u>declined</u> to include a religious school in a state program to improve playgrounds *(Trinity v Comer- 2017)*, then sent a case back for review when the Colorado Supreme Court blocked a tuition-scholarship program for students to attend private schools, including religious schools *(Douglas County v. Taxpayers for Public Education- 2017)*.

Pro choice is gaining momentum. Ohio has a huge pro choice program. Arizona, in 2017, made all 1.1 million public school students in the state eligible for a voucher program. In May of 2017 three families successfully challenged a Montana rule that prevented a voucher program from being used at religious schools. On July 26 of 2017 the Georgia Supreme Court unanimously upheld a program of tax credits for scholarships to some 13,000 students to attend private schools

There is a political dimension to the school choice movement as well. Public employee unions, and especially teacher unions, are a major bloc of the Democratic Party. The school choice movement is associated mainly with Republican office holders and their supporters.

Shifting union teaching jobs to the private sector reduces union membership and budgets. There will be less union money for political causes, fewer workers on political campaigns, less influence in decisions affecting education at all levels.

The federal level in the near future will be as pro choice as the current administration can make it.

The reader should understand that this movement towards alternatives to public schools is no mere disagreement over policy. Public school advocates feel that the school choice movement is hollowing out and draining needed funds from the public schools. They view school choice as an attack on public education itself, one of the bedrocks of our democracy. Pro choice advocates want the chance for their children to receive what they view as a better education than they would get in the local public school.

SIGNIFICANT OHIO CASES

Park Investment Company vs. Board of Tax Appeals

The Park Investment Company has received a degree of attention in Ohio far out of proportion to what would be expected by simply being the owner of a downtown Cleveland office building. The Park Investment Company, through litigation, changed the face of property assessment and taxation in Ohio.

The first Park Investment case was handed down by the Ohio Supreme Court in January of 1964. In this case Park claimed that commercial and industrial property in Cuyahoga County was over assessed. At that time commercial and industrial property was assessed for tax purposes at almost 50% of true value while other types of property were assessed at about 35% of true value. This situation was common throughout Ohio. Park claimed the disparity was unconstitutional. The Ohio Supreme Court agreed.

In response to the court decision, a common level of assessment for all classes of real property within each county and a basis for individual taxpayer appeals against discriminatory assessment were enacted into law in August of 1965. Since the first Park Investment case the Ohio Supreme Court has handed down three other supporting decisions.

A 1968 decision required a uniform level of assessment for all real property throughout the state and no longer permitted differences between counties. The 1971 decision declared a legislative plan to implement this concept unconstitutional while the final decision, in 1972, affirmed the constitutionality of implementing the uniform assessment rate over the normal six-year reappraisal cycle. The real property assessment rate is now 35% throughout the state.

The reader may wonder why the assessment rate is so important, why the Park Investment Company filed the lawsuit, and why the courts and the legislature have been struggling with this problem for years. As one humorist remarked, "Everyone believes in paying their taxes. It's in the assessment where the real fine work is done."

As shown in other chapters of this handbook, the Auditor's assessment of the SALE VALUE, the ASSESSMENT RATE and the TAX

RATE are all part of the equation to determine the TAXES OWED.
- Sale value x assessment rate x tax rate = taxes owed.
- Reducing any one of the three variables reduces the taxes owed.
- Increasing any one of the three variables increases the taxes owed.

DeRolph v. State of Ohio

From 1993 to 2002, the DeRolph case dominated the field of Ohio School finance. The "unconstitutional" label was placed on the Ohio system when the case reached the Ohio Supreme Court in the first of four DeRolph cases, (March 24, 1997) in a close 5-4 vote. The Ohio Legislature made great efforts to meet the mandates of the court. A significant effort was made to improve school funding and school buildings, the latter by creating and adequately funding the Ohio Schools Facilities Commission, now called the Ohio Facilities Construction Commission, described in a later section of this book. However the General Assembly never met all the mandates of the Court. That would have required a continuing increased financial commitment which they were unwilling to make. The Court was unwilling to force a showdown with the legislation by mandating compliance.

The struggle came to an end with the DeRolph 4 decision, handed down on December 22 of 2002. This decision, made before a new justice, recently elected, could form a new majority and change the direction of the court, said that the Ohio School Funding system was still unconstitutional, but "We refuse to encroach upon the clearly legislative function of deciding what the new legislation will be." In other words the Court, after making a strong effort over almost 10 years, gave up and agreed that public education in Ohio was a legislative function. Further, the court slammed the door on future litigation by stating, "No further jurisdiction over this particular case would be exercised, whether by this or any other court." The Ohio school funding system is still branded as unconstitutional and will remain so because the Court has prohibited any further litigation on this issue.

On June 24 of 2003 The Ohio Coalition for Equity and adequacy in School Funding, the plaintiffs in the DeRolph cases, attempted to move the case to the US Supreme Court. This effort was not successful. The Ohio Coalition and its tireless director, William L. Phillis, have been effective advocates for better public schools.

Community (Charter) Schools - Ohio PTA vs. State Board of Education

On October 25, 2006, in a 4-3 vote, the Ohio Supreme Court held that Chapter 3314 of the Ohio Revised Code, the state law authorizing establishment and operation of community or "charter" schools, is constitutional both on its face and as it was being applied in Ohio.

Advocates for Ohio's traditional public school systems, including the PTA, the Buckeye Association of School Administrators, the Ohio School Boards Association and others files suit on 2001 challenging the community school legislation enacted by the General Assembly.

Defendants were the State Board of Education, State Department of Education and other government offices and officials. A group of community school operators and White Hat Management, LLC, a company that manages 34 community schools located in various Ohio cities, joined in the defense.

The reader should note that when organizations such as the State Board of Education and Ohio Department of Education are named as defendants in a lawsuit such as this that these organizations and officials are mandated to carry out the laws enacted by the legislature. The public officials and members of these organizations do not necessarily agree with the laws they are mandated to implement and are defending in court.

Writing the majority opinion in this case, Judge Judith Ann Lanzinger rejected all constitutional arguments advanced by the community school opponents. Justice Lanzinger was joined in this opinion by Chief Justice Thomas J. Moyer and Justices Evelyn Lundsberg Stratton and Maureen O'Connell.

The majority opinion contained the following rationale, in pertinent part, to support the decision in favor of community schools:

- The General Assembly added to the traditional school system by providing more flexibility, parental choice and limited experimental educational programs in a deregulated setting. This action was within the authority of the General Assembly.
- Community schools had the same testing, graduation requirements and health and safety requirements as regular schools.
- Community schools provide a better chance for success to students whose needs might be better met in alternative school settings.
- The Legislature is justified in reducing state funding for the public school when enrollment decreases. When a student leaves, for any reason, the school district's funding is decreased and the district continues to receive full state funding based on the students actually enrolled.

- Funds derived locally are never taken from the local school district and redirected to the community schools.

Zelman V. Simmons-Harris –The School Voucher Issue

The Cleveland Scholarship and Tutoring Program was adopted by the Ohio Legislature in 1996. In this program, scholarship students received up to $2,500 to attend an "alternative school" or to hire private tutors. Parents were required to go to the alternative school and endorse the check, which assured that the money would be spent for education. The program was an attempt by the Ohio Legislature to provide alternative sources of education for children in the failing Cleveland schools. The thorny constitutional issue was that many of the alternative schools available to Cleveland children were Catholic schools.

In 1999 the Ohio Supreme Court ruled that the program did not violate the First Amendment regarding the establishment of religion. The crux of the Ohio decision was that "Money goes to religious institutions as a result of a 'genuinely independent private choice of individuals'" but the Court invalidated the program because it was adopted as part of the state budget in violation of the state constitution.

The legislature then quickly re-enacted the program as a separate bill, setting the basis for the legal challenges that followed.

Being unsuccessful at the state level, the case was filed in the United States District Court for the Northern District of Ohio. At this level the court ruled the program unconstitutional reasoning that it "advances religion" because most of the alternative school options available to Cleveland students were sectarian and no adjacent public schools had agreed to participate in the program. The 6th Circuit Court of Appeals affirmed.

The U.S. Supreme Court agreed to hear the case and, on June 27, 2002, the high court ruled that the State of Ohio was within it constitutional power to enact a school choice program for Cleveland's children. The majority reasoned that "neutral educational assistance programs that, like the program here, offer aid directly to a broad class of individual recipients defined without regard to religion" are constitutional. Further,"the Ohio program is neutral in all respects toward religion."

This, in the two above decisions the concepts of Community (Charter) schools and the type of educational voucher programs used in the Cleveland schools are both legal and permissible in Ohio.

Winkleman V. Parma City School District – IDEA litigation without an attorney

In this case the parents of a special education child contended that the Parma Schools failed to give their son a "free appropriate public education" as required by the Individuals with Disabilities Act (IDEA). The Winkleman's placed their child in a private school and petitioned a federal district court for reimbursement of expenses.

The U.S. Supreme Court agreed to take the case and on May 21 of 2007, in a 7-2 vote ruled that "A state must ... give 'any party' who objects to the adequacy of the education provided...the opportunity to present a complaint." IDEA gives parents independent, enforceable rights at the administrative stage, and it would be inconsistent with the statutory scheme to bar them from continuing to assert those rights in federal court at the adjudication state.

In a later ruling in the Winkelman case, decided on its merits, on June 2 of 2009 the U.S. Supreme Court declined to review the 6th U.S. Circuit Court of Appeals finding that Parma was not responsible for Jacob Winkelman's 2003-04 nearly $70,000 tuition bill at the Monarch school in Shaker Heights.

Hope Academy Broadway Campus v White Hat Management, Ohio Supreme Court, 2015

The Ohio Supreme Court, in 2006, ruled that legislation regarding charter schools, which the General Assembly called "Community Schools," was constitutional and that community schools are part of the state's public school system.

This case involved 10 Cleveland-area community schools that contracted with White Hat Management to operate the schools. During the term of the contract, seven of the ten schools had serious academic issues. Two were completely shut down for poor performance. When the contract expired the schools wanted to change management companies. Over the term of the contract 90 million dollars in state money had been funneled to White Hat Management to operate the schools, part of which was spent on equipment and other assets.

White Hat Management then claimed that the assets of the community schools, all bought with public funds, belonged to White Hat Management according to the terms of the contract which White Hat signed with the community schools. If the schools wanted the assets back, they would have to pay White Hat Management for them. The schools sued White Hat Management.

Perhaps holding its collective noses, a split 5-4 court agreed that the schools had willingly agreed to all terms of the contract. The contract was enforceable. White Hat owned the assets. If the schools wanted the assets back, they would have to pay White Hat for them.

A dissenting opinion by Justice O'Neill said "The only part of that contract that was fulfilled was that White Hat thoroughly and efficiently received the $90 million. There has been no quality education, there has been no safeguarding of public funds, and there most certainly has been no benefit to the children." O'Neill felt that the contract should not be enforceable because it "permits any operator who is providing a substandard education to squander public money and then, upon termination for poor performance, reap a bonus, paid for by public money."

Perhaps the lesson here is that when the relatively benign world of education, whose main purpose is helping people, intersects with the private sector, whose primary purpose is making money, an excess of caution on the part of those who represent education is appropriate.

Arming School Employees

On June 23, 2021 the Ohio Supreme Court handed down its decision on Gabbard V Madison Local School Distrist Board of Education, involving the arming of school district employees.

In 2018 the Madison Board of Education, following a shooting at one of its schools in 2016, passed a resolution allowing certain school employees to carry a weapon on school property, with the aim of protecting students, after receiving 24 hours of training.

A group of parents filed suit claiming that the Board's action was in violation of ORC 109.78 which states who must have police officer training and/or experience before they can be armed.

In a 4-3 decision, majority opinion written by Chieft Justice Maureen O'Conner, the court decided that the "or other position" of the ORC 109.78 was ruling in this case and did apply to school employees.

Accordingly, a school board can no longer authorize a staff member to be armed while on duty unless the staff member has either completed 728 hours of approved police officer training or has 20 years of experience as a peace office.

HB 99, currently before the Legislature, would exempt certain board authorized school employees from the peace officer training and experience requirement.

Related School Financial Factors

Phantom revenue

The phantom revenue effect occurs when the state attributes local income to school districts which they do not actually receive and reduces state aid accordingly. School leaders, as may be expected, object to this. It has become a public relations problem for the legislature. In HB 49 phantom revenue is now embedded in the state share index. Districts outside certain parameters in the median income and property value indexes will suffer from the phantom revenue effect..

Types of property – shifts in the tax burden

A major share of financial support for local schools in Ohio is raised by taxing property located within the school district. In fact, a major equity factor cited by the Ohio Supreme Court in the DeRolph cases is an over reliance on the local property tax to fund our schools.

Over time the Legislature has divided different types of local property into 3 categories. This has two advantages: (1) each class of property can be affected by different tax circumstances independently of the other classes and (2) the Legislature can deal with each class separately, especially in awarding tax breaks, without affecting the others.

The categories of property are as follows:
Class 1- Residential and Agricultural Real Property

This class consists of real estate (land and buildings) used as dwellings or in agriculture.

Note that a concept called Current Agricultural Use Value (CAUV) is applied to real property used in agriculture. Typically, real property is taxed at its "highest and best use." However, the true value for farmland is based upon the value of the land for farming, not what the land would be worth to a real estate developer or for some use other than farming. The farm home and an acre of ground around it are taxed at the residential rate. In a further break to farmers, tangible personal property, such as equipment and inventory used in farming, are not taxed at all.

These CAUV provisions are all intended to protect the family farm, to keep farmland from being gobbled up for development. They are also a reason why rural school districts have such low property valuations per pupil and so little to spend on the education of each pupil.

CAUV may also explain why you may see corn growing on expensive land in wealthy suburban areas or rented flocks of sheep grazing on the lawn at the headquarters site of a large corporation.

Note also that if residential property values grow at a greater rate than agricultural values, since they are both in the same class for tax purposes, homeowners will end up paying an increasing share of the school taxes assigned to that class and farm owners a decreasing share.

This class is assessed for tax purposes at 35% of real value. (See section on sale value, assessed value, reappraisals.)

Class 2- Commercial and Industrial Real Property

This class consists of real estate (land and buildings) used in business and industry. This class is assessed for tax purposes at 35% of real value.

Public Utility Tangible Personal Property Used in Business

Electric transmission and distribution personal property (T & D) is assessed at 85% of true value, electric production personal property at 24%, personal property of pipelines, water work and heating companies at 88% and rural T & D at 50%. Since most of these assets exist in wide geographic areas, there is an apportionment formula in the law (Senate Bill 3) which gives part of the tax money to every school district which contains public utility TTP. Utilities receive a tax break in that pollution control equipment is not taxed.

Tax reduction/20 mill floor

The law protects districts with low millage, prohibiting tax reductions below 20 effective mills as a result of reappraisals and re-adjustments from triennial updates. The 20 mills include a combination of all inside and effective outside mills.

Tax reduction factors (HB 920) are calculated separately for Class 1 (Residential and Agricultural) and Class 2 (all other) property. Thus, a district may be at the 20 mill floor for one class and not the other.

The 20 mill floor is important because, once the floor is reached, the HB 920 effect no longer applies to that district. In future reassessment and updates the district will receive an increase in income proportional to the tax duplicate.

In 1987, the General Assembly passed laws removing millage for joint vocational school districts from the 20-mill floor or guarantee and creating a separate two-mill floor for those districts. Also in 1987, the General Assembly removed emergency tax levy millage charged and payable in 1985 or thereafter from the 20-mill floor.

The chart below shows how the law treats various school issues in relation to both the tax reduction factors and the 20 mill floor.

COMMONLY USED SCHOOL LEVIES AND THEIR TREATMENT UNDER TAX REDUCTION FACTORS

Type of Levy	Subject to Reduction Factors	Factored in 20-Mill Floor Calculation
Inside Millage (Current Expense)	No	Yes
Inside Millage (Bond)	No	No
Inside Millage (Permanent Improvement)	No	No
Outside Millage (Current Expense)	Yes	Yes
Outside Millage (Bond)	No	No
Outside Millage (Permanent Improvement)	Yes	No
Outside Millage (Emergency)	No	No

There are currently 389 (about 63%) of Ohio districts at the 20 mill floor. HB 920 does not apply to these districts. Districts may be electing to raise additional funds using the kinds of tax issues to which the tax reduction factor does not apply. Once at the 20 mill floor, these districts will receive full value of all growth in property values on current expense millage when there is a reappraisal (every 6 years) or a triennial update.

The two most common ways districts can raise additional funds and still stay at the 20 mill floor are emergency levies for specific dollar amounts and income tax issues.

Deregulation of electric utilities

Though it is not generally known, regulated electric utilities in Ohio paid a much higher assessment rate on their property than other Ohio businesses, 100% of true value for production equipment and 88% for transmission and distribution property. Since the largest share of these taxes go to schools, every electric bill in the state contained a financial benefit to schools that few citizens knew or cared about.

Congress has passed legislation deregulating electric utilities. Ohio utilities could not compete financially if they had to pay a higher tax rate than competing suppliers from out of state. Our Legislature had to face the difficult problem of reducing the public utility tax rate without destroying the financial base of the school districts where major power plants were located.

In June of 1999 the Legislature passed Sub Senate Bill 3, which retained the assessment rate of transmission and distribution property at 88% (now 85%). By enacting a new kilowatt-hour tax, requiring the state to make up part of the loss in school district assessed value and phasing in the process, the Legislature intends to hold school districts financially harmless due to electric deregulation.

Educational Management Information System (EMIS)

In 1989 the Ohio Legislature created ORC 3301.0714, which required the State Board of Education to adopt rules for "a statewide Education Management Information System." A committee appointed by the State Superintendent completed the task. The EMIS framework and rules became effective in April of 1991.

Through EMIS, each school district in Ohio is required to provide a substantial amount of data to the ODE, in a uniform format, electronically. ODE compiles the data to show statewide, individual school district and individual school information in the categories required to be tracked. ODE then makes the information publicly available to the Legislature, to the school districts and the schools and to anyone who wants it.

ODE compiles a "report card" of the data, profiling each school within the district and the entire school district. State averages in the categories are also included for comparison purposes.

You can download the manual from the ODE as well as all data collected within the EMIS system. There you will find the categories and the data provided for each category. A sample few of the categories is given below:

- The number of students receiving each category of instructional service offered by the school district
- Details of the extracurricular program
- Student grades
- Student proficiency test scores
- Attendance, expulsion, suspension, corporal punishment, dropout and retention rates
- Number of Carnegie units taken by students
- Graduation rates

- Numbers and assignments of staff
- Student demographic data, including sex, race, poverty rates
- Costs, including administrative, support and extracurricular costs

With EMIS data, harnessed to the power of the computer, more statewide, school and school district educational and financial data are available than anyone could have dreamed of just a decade or more ago. This legislative solution for accountability in public education has opened wide the window of educational and fiscal operations in our public schools for all to see.

Uniform School Accounting System (USAS)

The Legislature and taxpayers of Ohio want a satisfactory level of fiscal accountability where their public schools are concerned. They wish to know WHERE the schools are spending the tax money and the RESULT of these expenditures. The first objective is much easier to accomplish than the second.

When you read your school district budget (appropriations resolution), you will find hundreds of areas of income and expenditure. These are called LINE ITEMS. At the left of each line item is a code number, with a brief explanation of what each line item is being used for. (Example "100 Employee's Salaries and Wages" or "500 Supplies and Materials")

Some of the codes are well known to building principals, who must code purchase orders. In the treasurer's office, the Uniform School Accounting System of coding is the Bible. It has to be. The law requires that the USAS be used in every school system in Ohio.

In 1975 the Ohio Legislature amended the Ohio Revised Code, section 117.05(B) to read:

"...the chief inspector and supervisor of public offices shall adopt and require within each school district the use of a uniform system of cost accounting whereby the direct and indirect of all districts' activities, including athletics and non-instructional activities, regardless of source of funding, can be analyzed."

Note the "can be analyzed" language.

The Legislature was mandating a system which:

A. Was uniform for every school district in the state.
B. Would allow anyone with knowledge of the system to track all financial transactions.
C. Allow analysis of financial data, and COMPARISONS BETWEEN DISTRICTS.
D. Make possible the statewide Education Management

Information System, which is discussed in a previous section.

With the USAS, school fiscal management began changing rapidly. Combined with EMIS, the Treasurer could no longer be a part-time staffer who came in on Monday mornings to sign purchase orders and checks and take care of the other details of the office. Now schools needed powerful computers for fiscal accounting. The district Treasurer's position has become a highly skilled one.

How does the USAS work? The staff of the Auditor of State, Ohio Department of Education, school district treasurers, and representatives from school-related organizations have produced, and periodically update, a user manual. The latest edition was available to schools in November of 1999. You can download the entire manual from the Internet.

The USAS is composed of SETS of numeric codes, called DIMENSIONS, each of which provides information. The dimensions are as follows:

TRANSACTION INDICATORS. Indicates the types of transactions which take place within a school district. The State Auditor assigns this dimension, primarily for computer purposes. This dimension may not appear in your school district budget.

FUNDS. Identifies the largest pools of money in the school district. It is a 3 digit code, which will appear first in the coding system. For example, 001 is the General Fund, the one used to operate the school district on a day-by-day basis. The bond retirement fund is 002. The permanent improvement fund is 003. The latest manual shows coding for 35 school district funds. The system allows for expansion up to 999 funds.

FUNCTIONS. This is a 4-digit code, which follows the 3-digit fund code. The code for the district-wide instructional program, paid for by the general fund (001) is 1000. There are four levels of coding under functions. Breaking the district-wide instructional program (1000) down further, there is 1200 (special education), 1220 (special instruction-handicapped) and 1222 special instruction handicapped - hearing impaired.

Note how the system moves us from general to more specific, from WHAT we are paying for to WHY we are paying for these things.

OBJECT. This is a 3-digit code focusing on "goods" or "services". With this dimension we can compare the cost-effectiveness of different computers or of providing services in-house or farming them out.

The system continues the delineation as shown.

Fund	Function	Object	Special Cost Center (where applicable)	Subject
XXX	XXXX	XXX	XXXX	XXXXXX

Operational Unit	Instructional Level	Job Assignment	Receipt Codes
XXX	XX	XXX	XXXX

There is a coding system for income and expenditures.

A school district is not required to use all the codes, provided it meets all local, state or federal reporting requirements.

This system does give a district the ability to determine, for example, the cost of teaching math in any grade or school, the cost of teaching math as compared with art, or the cost or supplies or materials in any school or subject area as compared to any other area.

Investing school funds

Most school districts in Ohio are multi-million dollar operations. Some large city budgets are in the hundreds of millions. Individual school district income and expense figures may not differ much at the end of the fiscal year. However, carryover financial balances and cash flow, when money is received and when it is needed to meet financial obligations, give districts the opportunity to operate sophisticated investment programs. Most do, with the result that interest income can be a significant part of the school budget.

Interest is the time value of money. It is wise to invest school funds for every DAY those funds are not needed to meet immediate financial obligations, and at the highest interest rate possible. Ohio law recognizes this by requiring that all school funds over $1,000 be deposited the next business day and all smaller amounts within 3 business days.

The Uniform Depository Act governs the investment of school district money.

In Ohio each school district must have an investment policy. Each Treasurer must receive in-service training on the subject of investing school funds or be restricted to investing only in Star Ohio and in certificates of deposit.

There are 4 generally accepted objectives which must be met in all school investments. They are:

1. Legality. School money must be invested only in approved instruments offered by approved institutions or agencies, with in approved time frames.

2. Safety. The major objective of the legal requirements is to provide as much assurance as possible that the principal and

interest will be safe. It will be returned to the school district without financial loss. The major way this is handled through the law is to require districts to invest in instruments backed by some agency of the state or federal government.

3. Liquidity. Liquidity means having funds available when they are needed to meet financial obligations. There is a general principle that the longer funds are invested, the higher the interest rate will be. You can see this at your bank as you compare the interest rates of the 3 month certificate of depos with the one-year CD. The one-year interest rate is usually higher.
In order to invest money for as long as possible, districts construct cash flow charts. Just as a simple example, using only two factors, the district may receive a payment of $1,000,000 from the County Auditor in late December. The payroll may be $250,000 per month. The Treasurer may use the first $250,000 to meet the January payroll and invest $250,000 of the money for one month, using this money to meet the February payroll, $250,000 for two months, using this money for the March pay roll and $250,000 for three months, using this money for the April payroll.

4. Yield. This last may surprise you. There is typically a close correlation between yield and risk. The higher the interest rate offered, the higher the risk. With public money, we are very risk adverse. Yield is the lowest of our 4 priorities.

The State of Ohio has developed an excellent investment program for public agencies called STAR OHIO. Most districts in Ohio use it. By pooling funds, STAR OHIO can make longer-term investments for up to one year. Because money is constantly moving in and out of the large fund, it also offers a high rate of liquidity to school districts. This program then offers high yield, high liquidity, low risk and legality all rolled into one. The Star Ohio number is 1-800-648-7827.
The Uniform Depository Act recognizes three kinds of school funds, available for investment, as follows:
1. Active funds. Money needed to meet current demands on the Treasury. The board selects the depository for active funds once every 5 years, after a public bidding process. This is usually a local bank, though a bank office in the district is not a requirement. The winning bidder may offer such benefits as free checking or "sweep" accounts, where all funds in all school

accounts are drawn down to zero each evening with the money being invested overnight. That's not a misprint. Financial instruments called repurchase agreements can be invested in for as short a period as overnight. That is really making each dollar work for the school district!

Winning bidders may provide a night depository for such items as cash from the Friday night athletic contest or play. Cash is dangerous to handle for many reasons. Local school officials are always eager to get cash safely into the bank as quickly as possible.

2. Interim funds. Money not needed currently, but needed before the period when they can be classified as Inactive Funds.

3. Inactive funds. Money not expected to be needed during the 5-year period of financial arrangement between the boards and the depository.

Chapter 135 of the Ohio Revised Code will provide more information to those who wish to explore school investments further.

Financial Threats and Alternatives to Public Schools

During the past few decades there has been a notable shift in public attitudes toward the cost and effectiveness of public services in general, and education in particular. There seems to be growing public criticism that our tax supported public schools are too expensive to operate, not as effective in educating our youth as the future will require, and cannot be made to respond to change or innovation which will address the above two issues.

In addition to an endless series of proposed changes grouped under the name of "reform," we are seeing efforts to weaken unions, which are viewed as the defenders of practices which many feel stand in the way of reform: tenure, seniority, the grid salary schedule and the disconnect between teacher pay and student success. At their annual convention in July of 2011, NEA secretary-Treasurer Becky Pringle called the situation "a new reality."

Another approach, which is expanding significantly, is to bypass the existing public schools completely, creating other venues for the education of our children and funding them with tax dollars. Alternatives to public schools share some common characteristics; they are typically non-union, which means that the owner/operators make all operational decisions and they cost about half as much per pupil to operate as public schools. Many of them are for-profit operations.

These approaches include scholarships (vouchers) and charter schools funded with tax dollars previously given to the public schools and transferred to the alternative school. When the students leave the public school, the tax money and the job of educating these students go with them.

A subset of charter school, eschools enroll about 30% of all charter students. They represent a new educational paradigm.

Traditional schools spend more money on the infrastructure supporting the classroom than they spend in the classroom. School facilities, student transportation, co-curricular activities, support personnel and services etc. are things eschool have little or nothing of and do not pay for. They also control staffing and salary decisions. They can be given half the tax money that public schools receive and their owners can still make a profit.

The Ohio Virtual Academy (OHVA) enrolled 13,000 students from throughout Ohio in 2013-14 and is growing. They received over $85.6 million in tax dollars from the state in that year and over $94.7 million when federal and other sources are counted.

The Electronic Classroom of Tomorrow is the largest in the state, with over 14,000 students. In 2017 they had over 2,000 graduates, which they claim to be the largest number for any single school in the country.

Choice is an attractive term to many people, freeing parents from the requirement of sending their children to their school and district of residence if more attractive taxpayer funded options can be made available. Choice vouchers are now being used by over Ohio 12,000 students at a taxpayer cost of over 46 million a year. These vouchers are intended to give students in poor performing districts an option of attending a better performing school. Current vouchers or scholarships are available for autistic students and Cleveland families with low incomes. The Jon Peterson Special Needs scholarships expands the autism program to include all categories of special needs students. There are currently 260,000 Ohio students who are on the special needs Individual Education Plans (IEPs).

There are still other options, such as post secondary options for high school students, giving them the ability to take college classes while still in high school and receive credit; home schooling; private and parochial schools, all of which drain money or students from the public schools.

It appears that the electronic age, financial considerations and changing attitudes toward education will make the future quite challenging for educators, legislators and citizens as we cope with incorporating these factors in to the basic task of educating our children.

Real Cost Per Pupil

Taking a big picture look, we can determine what a school district spends in a year, divide that by the ADM and get an average cost per pupil.

Increasing or decreasing the number of students in a class, school or school district and trying to determine the financial impact of that change in enrollment is a different story.

If you have 20 students in a classroom and increase the class size to 21 students, what is the cost of that additional student? You will need another desk, some textbooks and materials, but what other costs are increased? The teacher will probably be paid the same amount. The whole structure of the school system; land, buildings, support personnel, buses and equipment, contracts and agreements, bond issue payments, insurance, energy etc will not be increased. If the school district is given an additional $5,732 for that student it might be a good financial deal for the district. But what if that one student tips the balance and the district has to divide the class into two, or add another bus. That could be a $100,000 student.

Since the $100,000 student is rare and districts would go to great lengths to avoid that outcome, adding students and bringing cost per pupil money with them in most cases benefits the school district financially. Average cost per pupil for the district would be affected in a positive way since we have more students to divide into the budget which will increase very little, if at all, as a result of that additional student. District cost per pupil would come down.

Now let's reverse this process. Take away a student and the cost per pupil money. The teacher is still paid the same, as are all the support personnel. The bus still runs it's route. The whole structure of the school system will not be reduced. It would be the rare $100,000 student whose removal would drop the classroom size to a level which would allow the district to combine two classes into one, thus eliminating a teaching position and all of one classroom costs. The parents of those students affected are not going to like the larger class size so combination of two classes into one may not be politically feasible. Average cost per pupil would be affected in a negative way. There will be little or no reduction in school expenses as a result of the loss of that student. Cost per pupil will go up.

The current trend we are seeing in Ohio, to give students options to the public schools and to send the cost per pupil tax dollars with them to the new venue will likely result in an increase in cost per pupil in the public schools that the students leave. Further, good middle class jobs will go as well since alternatives to public schools do not generally provide employment packages which equal those of public schools.

Casino Profits and Schools

In 2009 the voters of Ohio approved a constitutional amendment permitting casino gambling. The amendment had failed several time previously. The great recession, which started in 2008, and which lead to high unemployment and the need for tax revenue, created the right conditions for passage of the amendment. Casino gambling proponents promised to create jobs and new tax revenue for schools and other government agencies.

Casinos pay 33% of their gross revenuc in taxes. Of this amount, 34% goes to schools in twice a year payments. Other agencies of government get the rest.. In Fy 2020 $96 million was distributed to traditional school fistricts, JVS and Technical Schools, and non-traditional schools; the latter includes community schools, charter schools preparatory schools, fitness and digital academies.

Tangible Personal Property Tax

The tangible personal property lax is a tax on items such as equipment used in manufacturing or business, machinery, inventories, furniture; items that can be touched and moved and are used in the conduct of business. As an example, all of the vehicles on an automobiles dealer's lot are tangible personal property, as is machinery used in manufacture. TPP does not include land or buildings or intangible assets such as money.

One of Ohio's most significant tax reforms in decades began in 2005, when the General Assembly launched a five year phase-out of the tangible property tax (HB 66) used in business with an overall 12 year phase out for school districts depending on the on the size of the revenue source. The goal of the tax cuts was to stimulate growth, particularly in manufacturing and, in the end, create jobs for Ohioans.

Earlier, in 1999-2000, deregulation of public utilities resulted in lower taxes for public utility tangible personal property for that segment of the Ohio economy (PUTP)

The tangible personal property tax income went mostly to school districts where the property was located. In many districts, particularly those with high industrial tax bases, the TPPT was a significant source of income. The Legislature then enacted a program of direct payments to school districts to replace the local TPPT with state money. This state reimbursement was originally to be phased out over 5 years.

In 2011 the payment program was modified by HB 153, and continued, based on how reliant districts were on TPPT. Lower reliant districts had their payments eliminated while they continued for high reliant districts.

The Tangible Personal Property Tax has ended for the majority of school districts and is phasing out for the few remaining districts where this was a major revenue stream.

Who is Watching the Money?
There was a time when Ohio school districts were small and uncomplicated. There was one school law expert in the entire state, Robert L. Drury, who worked for the Ohio Education Association. The Ohio School Boards Association thought they should have one so they hired the only prospective attorney in Ohio known to be specializing in the field of school law, Robert Baker. The Ohio revised code concerning schools was perhaps an inch thick. The school treasurer might be the board president's wife. Her job was to come to the office for an hour or so each week to sign checks.

Today school superintendents, treasurers and business managers, the three key officers dealing with school finance, are highly trained professionals. Treasurers with MBA degrees in accounting are common. School boards have realized that school systems are multi-million dollar businesses. Large districts may have yearly budgets of hundreds of million dollars. Excellent management is essential for success. Securing school income, managing it, accounting for every penny, spending it wisely, all while operating in the public eye and keeping the public informed and supportive requires high skill levels not found in many fields.

Covid19 Pandemic 2020:
The Covid 19 Pandemic impacted the entire world by late 2019 and by March 13, 2020 the State of Ohio was quarantined with only essential workers in action, including public schools. Governor DeWine provided daily updates on the progress of the virus and guidance on essential businesses to remain open during the State closure. Initially, Ohio public school districts were closed with minimal essential operations occurring to maintain operations; students and staff remained at home in order to minimize the spread of the virus.

This was truly an unprecedented event for Ohio public school districts; with many districts closed until further notice from the State of Ohio. During the closure, school districts cleaned and sanitized the buildings in preparation for the eventual return of staff and students. School districts also developed online programs to continue the educational process for students and the delivery of food for the Federal Breakfast and Lunch programs.

Governor DeWine signed HB 197 which waived State Testing requirements for school children, allowed school boards to meet electronically instead of in person, and most importantly established guidance on payroll for Ohio School District staff. HB 197 specifically stated that teachers can continue to be paid for online instructional services; while classified staff (bus drivers, secretaries, custodians, administration, and other non-teaching positions) will be paid based on being available to be called in to perform services. When staff were called in for services, the district would comply with the guidelines and requirements for proper social distancing, mask attire, and further protections such as shields based on the State of Ohio and Department of Health requirements.

School districts refined their online educational programs and the delivery of food services to students as the Pandemic progressed. The State of Ohio developed a color code system to identify counties with dangerous levels of Covid 19 cases that would recommend districts to remain closed and online for instructional services. The system allowed face to face instruction with proper social distancing and mask attire if the district was located in a county with moderate levels of Covid 19 cases based on the color code system. Many school districts returned with educational programs that allowed parents to enroll in pure online educational programs or hybrid programs with staggered face to face instruction combined with online programs in order to properly social distance. The 2020 school year ended with school districts being creative for graduation ceremonies including online events and drive thru car events where students and families remained in their respective cars. The 2021 school year ended with some students attending an entire school year online depending on the school district location.

Ohio School Finance in the Covid19 Era:

Federal and State programs assisted Ohio employees with stimulus and supplemental pay in order to assist employees as they remained at home in quarantine during the Pandemic. The Family Medical Leave Act (FMLA) was extended to include paid leave for employees that were exposed or infected by the virus. The Federal Government provided various stimulus checks to United States taxpayers. The State of Ohio provided supplemental unemployment benefits (an increase from normal unemployment benefits) to Ohio employees that became unemployed due to the Pandemic.

The Federal Government established three key acts of legislation to provide supplemental financial support to public schools throughout the nation during the Pandemic:

1. Coronavirus Aid, Relief and Economic Security (CARES) Act
2. Coronavirus Response and Relief Supplemental Appropriations (CRRSA) Act
3. American Recovery Plan (ARP) Act

Coronavirus Aid, Relief and Economic Security (CARES) Act

The CARES Act passed on March 27, 2020 provided funding to Ohio schools through four programs: Elementary & Secondary School Emergency Relief (ESSER), Coronavirus Relief Fund (CRF), Broadband Ohio Connectivity Grant, and Governor's Emergency Education Relief (GEER). The CARES Act allocated $657.7M in Federal funding to Ohio schools. All of the Federal grants are funded through the Ohio Department of Education (ODE) Comprehensive Continuous Improvement Plan (CCIP) system for grant funding. The CCIP system is utilized for the application and verification of grants; where districts submit budgets ultimately authorized by the ODE and then request reimbursement for actual expenditures from the ODE via the grant funding.

Elementary & Secondary School Emergency Relief (ESSER) Funds

The first round of ESSER funding for Ohio districts (ESSER 1) was based on the amount of Title 1 funding that the district receives, authorized by the CARES Act ($489.2M to Ohio schools). The grant provided funding for Title 1 expenditures, expenditures directly related to the Pandemic, and operational expenditures to maintain a continuity of services. The allowance for continuity of services provided school districts great flexibility in spending the grants; which is not normally the case in regards to grant funding for school districts. Allowable expenditures were also retroactive to March 13, 2020 in order to capture the additional expenditures that school districts encountered due to the Pandemic. Expenditures will be funded until September 30, 2022. The amount each district received was proportionate to overall district Title 1 revenue; districts that receive major revenue streams for Title 1 had substantial ESSER 1 grant funding.

Coronavirus Relief Fund (CRF)

The Coronavirus Relief Fund was authorized by the CARES Act providing $100M in funding to Ohio schools for expenditures incurred due to the public health emergency due to COVID19 covering the period of March 1, 2020 to December 2020. The allocation was based on enrollment, special populations, and transportation costs of each district.

Broadband Ohio Connectivity Grant

The Broadband Ohio Connectivity Grant was authorized by the CARES Act providing $50M in funding to Ohio schools for specific expenditures primarily related to internet connections for students, hotspots and public Wi-fi infrastructure. This was due to the requirements for students and staff to learn and instruct from home via online learning connections via home computers.

Governor's Emergency Education Relief (GEER)

The GEER grant was authorized by the CARES Act providing $18.5M in funding to Ohio Educational Service Centers, county boards of developmental disabilities, Ohio School for the Blind and Ohio School for the Deaf. The grants are for expenditures from March 13, 2020 until September 30, 2022. Funds were allocated by enrollment and flat amounts for the Ohio School for the Blind and Ohio School for the Deaf.

Coronavirus Response and Relief Supplemental Appropriations (CRRSA) Act

The CRRSA Act passed December 27, 2020 provided a total of $1.99B in ESSER funding to Ohio schools. This is the second round of ESSER funding for Ohio districts referred to as ESSER 2 funding. Each Ohio school district allocation is based on the total Title 1 funds the district usually receives. The ESSER 2 funding was greater than ESSER 1 funding since ESSER 2 is based on 100% of regular Title 1 funding that the district receives. Allowable expenditures included the same ESSER 1 allowable usage and expanded to expenditures addressing learning loss, preparing buildings for reopening, and projects to upgrade air quality in buildings. Again, the expenditures are retroactive to March 13, 2020 with an expiration of September 30, 2023.

American Rescue Plan (ARP) Act

The ARP Act passed March 11, 2021 will provide a total of $4.5B in ESSER funding to Ohio schools. This is the third round of ESSER funds (ESSER 3). The ESSER 3 funds have similar allowable expenditures as ESSER 2 and most school districts will receive substantial amounts of funding from ESSER 3 since the ARP Act is by far the largest of the three acts for Federal funding supplements due to the Pandemic. The CARES Act provided $657.7M in grant funding to Ohio, while the CRRSA Act increased the overall funding to Ohio with $1.99B. The ARP

Act is the largest of the three ESSER funds with $4.5B going to Ohio Schools. ESSER 3 funds are for allowable expenditures from March 13, 2020 to September 30, 2024.

New Expenditures due to the COVID19 Pandemic

Ohio School Districts will strategically utilize the supplemental funds listed above to cover the additional costs due to various impacts from the Pandemic. Preparing the schools for reopening and the requirements for safe learning environments has added new expenditures to Ohio school districts such as: desk shields, masks, sanitization equipment, sanitization supplies, temperature scanners and social distance signage. Online operations have added new expenditures for online meeting subscriptions such as ZOOM, online educational platforms, one to one technology and the expansion of internet capacity of the school district. Last but not least, learning loss is a very important expenditure that will substantially increase as school districts address the needs of students after the quarantine periods. Many school districts are getting creative with extended school years, extended school days, credit recovery and summer school programs to address learning loss. The supplemental funding will provide additional funds for districts to increase teaching staff in order to increase intervention programs and decrease student to teacher ratios in order to address learning loss. If State Funding for public schools remains consistent avoiding any decreases, the Federal investment in Ohio's scholars can really make a difference for the disruption of public education due to the Pandemic.

Conclusion – Get Involved

Ohioans have learned the bitter truth that their schools cannot be taken for granted. Free public education for the children of this state is not a principle established forever. Rather, it is a condition which must be reestablished, resold, and rewon with each local school election and state legislative session.

Ohio schools look for their survival to public support and approval. The vote on school issues is one which affects the lives of great numbers of young people. Over the decades, the accumulated effect of many local elections and legislative sessions, as manifested in the quality of the schools, influences the course of the entire society.

No citizen has the moral right to be ignorant on school matters.

Schools are public business. Information concerning many school matters will come to you through the newspapers, postal system, radio, television, by word-of-mouth, from students. If you want information which you have not received through these channels, call the office of your individual school or the administrative offices of the school district and you will receive the information you seek.

School employees are public servants. This does not mean that they will permit themselves to be abused, harassed or insulted. It does mean that you need never fear to call any school employee and ask information or assistance. You will not be intruding. Don't be shy. The typical school person is eager to be of assistance.

School board members are public representatives. They live right in your school district. Board members are generally active community citizens, eager to hear your views and accessible so you can easily present them. Since the school board stands at the head of your school system, board members have access to a broad range of information about the schools. Further, they are in an excellent position to bring suggestions to the school official who can do something about them. Give your board members a chance to serve you.

School board meetings are open to the public. Regular meetings are held once or twice a month, according to a regular schedule. All official school business must be acted upon by the board of education in full view of the public. The Sunshine Law requires it. Any citizen in attendance may address the board of education, although permission may have to be obtained in advance. Attend school board meetings.

You will get a good idea of how the schools are operated after several meetings. There might even be a question or two you want answered "from the top."

PTA and other parent group meetings are open to the public. This is a good chance to meet school people and parents. The schools often use PTA meetings as vehicles for distributing information. You can also ask questions. The whole aura of a PTA meeting is less formal and more personal than a school board meeting, but just as effective in allowing you to get involved in school matters.

Your school probably mails out a monthly newsletter which is filled with information about school goings-on. If you get it, read it. If you don't, call the office and get on the mailing list.

There are so many sources of school information available to the public that no citizen needs be misinformed or ill-informed on school matters. The schools are eager to provide you with information.

The existence of Ohio public schools depends upon the soundness and integrity of your judgment on school issues. This in turn must be based upon an adequate understanding of the financial operation of our schools. Your responsibility as an Ohio citizen requires that you get involved and get the facts.

Glossary of Terms

Assessment Rates: The percentage of true value that determines the taxable value of property. The rate is 35% in Ohio.

Average Daily Membership (ADM): The pupil count used in determining basic aid.

Bond Levy: A levy to pay the debt service on bonds. The tax rate is set annually to generate the amount of money necessary to meet debt service obligations. These levies are not subject to reduction factors and do not figure into the calculation of the 20-mill floor.

CAUV: Certain qualifying agricultural property has its true value determined based on its current agricultural use rather than on its highest and best use. CAUV measures the ability of the land to provide farm income.

Class One Real Property: Property classified as residential or agricultural. This includes residential rental property with three or fewer units.

Class Two Real Property: Property classified as commercial, industrial, or mineral. This includes residential rental property with four or more units.

Current Expense Levy: Inside or outside millage used for current expenses of a school district.

Effective Tax Rate: The tax rate charged on real property after application of tax reduction factors.

Emergency Levy: A voted levy for a period not to exceed five years that must generate a single dollar amount in each of those five years.

Fiscal Year: The fiscal year is the term of operation year for public school districts which runs from July 1 to June 30. The term is often interchangeable with "school year". School districts operate on a fiscal year while most local governments such as cities and counties operate on the calendar year.

Homestead Exemption Credit: Elderly and disabled homeowners with incomes under 31,800 in 2017 (indexed for inflation beginning in 2000) are eligible for a tax credit based on their income level and home value. The cost of this credit is reimbursed to local governments by the state.

Inside Mills: Millage levied under the 10-mill limitation in the constitution. Such millage is enacted without a popular vote and is not subject to tax reduction factors. Schools typically receive about half of this millage.

Market Value: The value of real property determined by its price on an open market.

Mill: One-tenth of one percent.

Outside Mills: Millage levied in addition to inside millage. Such millage can only be levied after an affirmative popular vote.

Permanent Improvement Levy: A restricted use levy that can only be used for capital-related expenses.

Public Utilities (for property tax purposes only): Electric companies, gas companies, local and long-distance telecommunications companies (including paging and cellular), pipelines, heating companies, water transportation, waterworks, and railroads.

Qualifying Millage: The property tax rate that must be levied for a school district to qualify to receive state basic aid. The rate is 20 mills. Included in the 20 mills are all current expense levies (using the rate before application of reduction factors), emergency levies, current expense levies of overlapping joint vocational districts, and the millage equivalent of current expense income taxes.

Real Property: Land and buildings.

Reappraisal: A process completed every six years by county auditors to determine the market value of all real property. It is accomplished through a visual inspection of all property.

Recognized Value: Taxable property values adjusted to phase-in the impact of valuation increases due to reappraisal or triennial update. This concept is only used in the calculation of basic aid.

Tax Capacity: The ability to raise revenue from a given tax base. It is the revenue that can be generated per pupil from a one-mill tax.

Tax Effort: In general, the burden of taxation on a taxpayer. It is the percentage of income in a school district that is paid for residential and agricultural property taxes and school district income taxes.

Tax Rate: The rate of a tax levy before application of tax reduction factors. This is the rate charged on all taxable tangible personal property.

Tax Reduction Factor: The amount that a tax levy rate has been reduced to prevent the levy from producing more revenue due to reappraisal or triennial update.

Tax Year: An annual accounting period for tax purposes that consists of 12 consecutive months. The tax year for property taxes, as well as individual income taxes for most taxpayers, is the calendar year January 1 to December 31.

Taxable Value: The value of property subject to taxation, after application of assessment rates.

Ten Percent Credit: A 10% tax credit (rollback) is granted to residential property owners that are non-business property. The cost of this credit is reimbursed to the local government by the State. This credit was repealed by HB59 for new and replacement levies on the November 2013 election thereafter.

Triennial Update: A process that occurs three years after reappraisal to update the market value of all real property. It is accomplished through studies of property transactions since reappraisal.

True Value: The market or book value of property. For real property, it is market value. For business tangible and non-electric production utility tangible property, it is depreciated cost. For electric production equipment, it is 50 percent of original cost.

Two and a Half Percent Credit: Owner occupied residential properties receive a 2.5% tax credit (rollback). The loss of this credit is reimbursed to the local government by the State. This credit was repealed by HB59 for new and replacement levies on the November 2013 election thereafter.

20-Mill Floor: A school district with at least 20 mills of current expense taxes levied may not have its effective tax rate reduced below 20 mills. Once the effective tax rate reaches 20 mills, no further reductions in effective rates are made, allowing such districts to receive the full impact of increases in taxable values on those mills.

Glossary terms taken primarily from "Property Taxation and School Funding," by Meghan Sullivan and Mike Sobul, Section Chief, Tax Analysis Division, Ohio Department of Taxation, February 2010, revised and supplemented by Robert Stabile.

Note: This handbook is a basic primer. This edition has been expanded and updated. Ohio school finance laws are complex. This text attempts to provide a "big picture" look at the subject. Not every finance detail important to a practitioner in the field could be included here and still make this an easy-to-read and understandable handbook. Therefore, this handbook should not be the sole guide for school district decision making; nor does it present legal advice.

This book is written without footnotes, again for simplicity. On occasion source materials are provided in the text. Much information was provided by the experts in various related fields listed on page 2 of the book. All information provided is the latest available to the author. To obtain information about source materials not shown in the book, email RGStabile@aol.com.